A New Look
at Christian
Morality

Fides Publishers, Inc., Notre Dame, Ind.

A New Look at Christian Morality

Charles E. Curran

Christian Morality Today II

71 - 33

Preface

This book comprises eight chapters and an epilogue which consider many of the critical questions in moral theology today. Most of the chapters were originally written as theological studies of particular questions in moral theology. The basic theological approach to the different questions under consideration gives a unity to the book as a whole. An epilogue tries to summarize and synthesize the most important themes and approaches which have been mentioned in the other chapters. I would like to thank the publishers and periodicals listed below for their kind permission to reprint materials which first appeared in their publications. Above all, I want to take this opportunity to publicly express my deep appreciation to my friends and to the faculty and student body of The Catholic University of America for their support and encouragement.

Acknowledgments

The Commonweal, for "The Relevancy of the Ethical Teaching of Jesus"; *The Catechist,* for the first part of "Conversion: The Central Moral Message of Jesus"; Charles Scribner's Sons, for "Absolute Norms in Moral Theology," which originally appeared in *Norm and Context in Christian Ethics,* ed. Paul Ramsey and Gene H. Outka; The Canon Law Society of America, for "Church Law and Conscience," which originally appeared in *Law for Liberty,* ed. James E. Biechler (Helicon, 1967); The John Knox Press, for "The Moral Theology of Bernard Häring," which originally appeared in *The New Day,* copyright M. E. Bratcher, 1968; Joseph F. Wagner, for "Dialogue with Joseph Fletcher," which originally appeared in the *Homiletic and Pastoral Review; The Proceedings of the Catholic Theological Society of America,* for "Masturbation and Objectively Grave Matter."

Contents

The Relevancy of the Ethical Teaching of Jesus

Chapter One

Contemporary theology has shifted its gaze from heaven to earth, from God to man, from the after life to the present life. Human existence and its meaning are the primary problems of contemporary theology. The world today is ageric—modern man is not a contemplator but a doer. Dogma and speculation for its own sake have very little appeal to man today. Within the Catholic Church some are questioning the primacy attributed to liturgy over life itself. Is liturgy not the celebration of life rather than the font and source of all life? Life is the most important reality.

The Christian Church and the individual Christians are reading the signs of the times. Christians need to speak to the actual life of man today. What does the ethical teaching of Jesus mean for contemporary human existence? But the Church must carefully avoid just talking. Words without deeds are like the Pauline sounding brass or tinkling cymbal. The credibility gap merely widens when the pious mouthings of the Church are contradicted by its own life and actions.

The Christian trying to realize the meaning of human life naturally turns to the ethic of Jesus. The ethical teaching of Jesus is not a detailed blueprint for human activity, but the follower of Jesus at least begins his quest by examining the ethical teaching of the scriptures. Many speculative problems arise from a consideration of biblical ethics and modern existence. Theology today is discussing secularity, the relationship between the immanent and the transcendent, the connection between human progress and the coming of the kingdom, the meaning of history. An older theology struggled with the problems of nature and grace or law and gospel. A thorough consideration of all these issues lies beyond the scope of the present chapter. The essay will merely attempt to indicate the relevancy of the ethic of Jesus for the contemporary Christian.

AN ETHIC OF LOVE

What is the ethical teaching of Jesus? In general, Jesus calls his followers to live a life in union with God and neighbor. Many theologians summarize the moral teaching of Jesus under the category of love. The three synoptic accounts mention the twofold commandment of love of God and neighbor as the core of the ethical teaching of Jesus (Mark 12:28-34; Matt 22:34-40; Luke 10:25-37).

Why is the twofold love commandment called a new commandment? Love of God and neighbor was central in the teaching of the Old Testament and in many other religions. One distinctive characteristic of the love ethic of Jesus is the insistence on an indissoluble interior bond between the love of God and the love of neighbor. The follower of Jesus is recognized by his love for others. The judgment scene of

Matt 25 indicates that man's relationship to God is known and manifested in his relationship with his fellow man. The follower of Jesus cannot claim to love God and yet neglect his neighbor who is hungry, thirsty, naked, alone, or in prison. John says very poignantly that man cannot love the God he does not see if he does not love the neighbor whom he does see (1 John 4:20). The ethic of Jesus does not eschew life in this world; rather, the authentic love of God is found in a loving concern for others. The follower of Jesus can find no excuse (not even worship at the altar) which takes precedence over his loving concern and forgiveness for his neighbor.

A second characteristic of the love ethic of Jesus centers on the universality attached to the concept of neighbor. To love friends is easy. To love when one is loved in return requires no self-giving. But the Christian love for others is modeled on the love of Jesus for us. Jesus loved us while we were yet sinners. Jesus' love for us did not depend on what we could give him in return. The love of Jesus is completely disinterested and gratuitous in the sense that his love in no way depends on the loving qualities or the response of men. Jesus' love is creative, not responsive; giving, not possessing. Who are the privileged recipients of the love of Jesus? The strong, the influential, the wealthy, the intelligent, the respected? No, the privileged recipients of Jesus' love are the poor, the children, and even sinners. The non-value of the recipients of the good news of salvation is a startling fact.

The Christian is called to love just as Jesus has loved. The greatest example of Christian love is love for enemies. The enemy can give the lover nothing in return. In fact, the enemy returns hatred for love. The enemy might react with vengeance and annoyance, but love of enemies remains the great sign of Christian love. Our love for others does not depend on what they can do for us. Since the love of Jesus does not depend on the loving qualities of others, the object of his love is universal. The parable of the good Samaritan illustrates the universality of neighbor in the love ethic of Jesus. The neighbor is the person who is in need. The priest and the levite walk by the man in the road; but the Samaritan, a foreigner and enemy, has compassion on the man in need. Love is not just liking but a loving concern for the neighbor in need.

Perhaps the ethical teaching of Jesus as the complete giving of self to God and neighbor cannot be perfectly expressed in any human formula or concept. There are theological difficulties in reducing the ethic of Jesus even to the twofold commandment of love of God and neighbor. The love of the Christian for his God and his love for his neighbor are not the same kind of love. Love of God is the adoring gratitude of one who has received all from the giver of life. Love of neighbor is a creative giving and a redemptive forgiving which does not depend on the lovable qualities of the other. The two loves are different. The scriptures seldom speak of man's love for God as *agape* precisely because of the difference between God's love for man and man's love for God.

Even man's relationship to his neighbor cannot be adequately explained in terms of *agape*—the loving concern which is a total giving independent of the lovable qualities of the other. The human relationship of love does at times require that I love the other precisely because of his loving qualities. A human person does want to be loved in himself and for what he is. Bishop Pike has criticized Professor Fletcher for reducing the entire Christian ethic to *agape*. There are times when *eros* as a responsive and possessive love or friendship as a mutual love are absolutely essential for human well-being. The theologian should be cautious in thinking that he can reduce the ethical teaching of Jesus to any neat human formulae. H. Richard Niebuhr claims that no human virtue as such can adequately explain the ethical teaching of Jesus.

However, all can agree that the ethical teaching of Jesus calls for the giving of self to God and neighbor. The neighbor in need, according to many biblical passages, has the first claim on the love of the Christian. We must examine this ethical teaching in more detail. The most prolonged statement of the ethical teaching of Jesus is found in the composite arranged in Matthew around the literary form of the Sermon on the Mount (Matt 5-7). Luke brings together much of the ethical teaching of Jesus in his shorter Sermon on the Plain (Luke 6:20-49). Matthew begins the Sermon on the Mount with the beatitudes. Although Luke employs the beatitudes in a sapiential perspective and the more primitive form of the beatitudes was probably a messianic proclamation, Matthew employs the beatitudes in a catechizing and moralizing way to outline the characteristics which mark the life of the follower of Jesus. Matthew's spiritualization of the beatitudes (the poor in spirit and the clean of heart) and the peculiar emphasis on justice or righteousness indicate that Matthew is trying to describe the moral life of the follower of Jesus. The Christian is called to be the light of the world and the salt of the earth through love, meekness, mercy, forgiveness, peacemaking, and the pursuit of righteousness.

Matthew then continues to describe the ethical teaching of Jesus as the completion and fullness of the law. Matthew first contrasts (perhaps by way of completion and not antithesis according to W. D. Davies) the ethical teaching of Jesus with that of the Scribes, the theologians of the time. The six antitheses or completions of the ethical teaching of Jesus concern anger, chastity, divorce, oaths, forgiveness and love of enemies. The section ends with a call to be perfect just as our heavenly Father is perfect. The parallel verse in

Luke is a call to be merciful or compassionate as our heavenly Father is merciful (Luke 6:36). Matthew begins Chapter 6 by comparing the attitude of the Pharisees and the
followers of Jesus on the matters of almsgiving, prayer, and
fasting. The follower of Jesus is concerned with a true change
of heart and not just a rigid external observance. In the final
section of the Sermon on the Mount, Matthew outlines other
characteristics of the followers of Jesus. Jesus asks for a complete and loving trust in himself which leads to the aban-
donment of all other persons and things. Thus the literary
device of the Sermon on the Mount capsulizes the ethical
teaching of Jesus as found throughout the New Testament.

EMBARRASSING QUESTIONS

A meditative reflection on the moral teaching of Jesus
raises embarrassing questions. Do the Church and the followers of Jesus really put into practice the ethical teaching
of their Lord? Can the Church truly say to Jesus: "When you
were hungry, thirsty, naked, lonely, abandoned, and in
prison, I was there to comfort you"? Does the average person
living today see reflected in the life of the Church the ethical
teaching of Jesus? Is the primary concern of the Church the
neighbor in need or is the Church more interested in preserving and augmenting its image, status, wealth, and power?
Is the Church truly credible when it does raise its voice on
particular issues, since so often there is only loud silence on
other problems involving the neighbor in need? Has the
Church left all to follow Jesus or is it trying to serve two
masters? When the hierarchical Church does speak on a particular issue, how often are the words accompanied by appropriate actions even to the giving away of earthly power
and possessions? Does the Church really take seriously the
ethical teaching of Jesus?

However, one cannot merely point an accusing finger at the Church. How about myself as a Christian? Am I really willing to give all that I possess for my neighbor in need? Am I really willing to forgive my enemies the same way that Christ did? How difficult it remains to speak well of those who have hurt me in the past. Am I always willing to turn the other cheek or to walk an extra mile? How often do I really go out of my way to help others?

There exists an even more embarrassing question: can anyone be expected to live the ethical teaching of Jesus? At first glance, all are compelled to admit the beauty and sublimity of the ethical teaching of Jesus. But the moral demands of Jesus are radical and seemingly impossible. The disciple of Jesus leaves all things to follow his master. Luke, who is the evangelist of total renouncement, even goes so far as to call for hatred of father and mother, brother and sister (Luke 15:26-33). Can anyone truly live the ethical teaching of Jesus?

The ethic of Jesus seems totally unreal when applied to the particular problems that so often arise in our lives. How can a Christian not worry about what he is going to eat or drink? What minister of God's Word would ever say to an improvident father that he should not worry about food, clothing, and shelter for his family? Can a wife forgive her husband and welcome him with open arms if he constantly beats her and the children? Can I as a Christian stand by and turn the other cheek when other innocent people (e.g., young children) are being attacked? How practical is it not to resist the evil doer? Who can possibly give to everyone who asks? Is the gospel injunction of turning the other cheek an apt solution to the complicated problems of American involvement in Vietnam? In all wars?

Even the Church does not follow the ethical demands of Jesus. Just after speaking about divorce, Matthew reminds the followers of Jesus never to take any oaths but to restrict their speech to yes and no (Matt 5:33-37). However, the Roman Catholic Church has insisted on a number of oaths that must be taken by priests and teachers. Even on such a practical matter as judicial processes and matrimonial courts, Church procedure is practically never willing to accept the word of the Christian. The ethic of Jesus might be sublime and beautiful, but the teaching of Jesus seems impossible and irrelevant for the daily life of Christians.

PROPOSED SOLUTIONS

Conscientious Christians have constantly grappled with the problems created by the ethical teaching of Jesus. A true follower of Jesus cannot dismiss his whole ethical teaching as irrelevant and meaningless for daily human existence. Some explain the difficulty connected with the moral teaching of Jesus as arising from the fondness for imagery and exaggeration, which is associated with the Oriental mentality. The beam in one's eye, the camel and the eye of the needle, forgiveness seventy times seven times, all these expressions embody overstatement and exaggeration. Undoubtedly Jesus reflected the thought patterns of his own culture, but can the entire moral teaching of Jesus be satisfactorily explained in terms of Oriental exaggeration? Within a Lutheran tradition some want to interpret the Sermon on the Mount as *Moyses Moysissimus*—the law of Moses in the nth degree. The important function of law is to bring man to acknowledge his own weakness and sinfulness. The Mosaic Law brought man to Christ not by continuous development, but through discontinuity. The Law made man aware that he could find salvation not in the works of the Law but only through faith in Christ Jesus. The radical and impossible demands of the Sermon on the Mount only intensify the function of law which brings man to realize his sinfulness and need of redemption through faith in Christ. Although such a solution does serve as a partial explanation of the problem, the *Moyses Moysissimus* solution does not really take seriously the ethical teaching of Jesus.

A few have tried to take literally the ethical teaching of Jesus as universal norms for moral conduct which are always and everywhere binding. Such biblical fundamentalism quickly clashes with the problems of everyday human existence. Common sense and experience remind us that man cannot accept the ethical teachings of Jesus as laws of conduct which are always obliging in similar circumstances.

The Catholic theological tradition has generally ignored the problem created by the radical ethical demands of Jesus. At least on a popular level, Catholic teaching maintained that only a few people were called to perfection. Such people followed the evangelical counsels and generally entered the religious life. The vast majority of men living in the world were content with just observing the commandments which are binding on all men. Catholic theology thus ignored the problem created by the radical moral teaching of Jesus. However, the consequences of ignoring the problem have been evident in Catholic life and practice. Only with Vatican II does popular Catholic teaching stress the universal vocation of all Christians to perfection. Catholic theology has not developed a theology and spirituality for life in the world because people outside the religious life were content with just obeying the commandments.

Many serious attempts to come to grips with the radical ethical teaching of Jesus hinge on the question of eschatology. Interestingly, contemporary theologians are also calling for a renewed eschatology. The eschatological views see the ethic of Jesus in connection with his mission in proclaiming the reign of God. The ethic of Jesus is above all a religious ethic, intimately connected with the reign that Jesus proclaimed. The reign of God calls for a complete and radical response from the hearer.

Albert Schweitzer well represents the school that labeled the moral teaching of Jesus an "interim ethic." In reacting against liberal Protestantism, Schweitzer stressed the eschatological dimension of Jesus' mission. Jesus expected the kingdom of God to come even before his disciples returned from their first missionary journey. When the kingdom did not come, Jesus went up to Jerusalem to precipitate the coming of the kingdom by his death. The strenuous ethic proposed by Jesus was for the very short interim that would precede the final coming of the kingdom. The ethical teaching of Jesus cannot be lived and sustained over a long period of time. Jesus' ethic is intimately connected with his own mistaken eschatology. Today, most theologians have rejected the opinion proposed by Schweitzer. The reign of God is not all future; to some extent the kingdom of God in Christ is already present and working in the world. Even many who maintain that Jesus believed in a very quick coming of the final stage of the reign of God do not think that Jesus would have preached a different ethic even if he had realized that the final stage of the kingdom would not arrive for a long period of time.

Perhaps the ethic of Jesus was meant only to describe life in the final stage of the reign of God and has no practical meaning for life here and now. Jesus did not propose a moral teaching for life in this world but was merely describing the life in the final coming of the reign of God. Again there is some truth in such an assertion, but the follower of Jesus cannot conclude that the ethical teaching of the master is completely irrelevant for Christians living in the world of today. Even the conflict and troubling situations described by Jesus seem much more applicable to the situation of our own daily lives than to the description of some future state of blessedness.

ESCHATOLOGICAL TENSION

The ethic of Jesus is closely alligned with his mission in proclaiming the reign of God. The final stage of the reign of God is coming. The reign is already begun but is now hastening toward its conclusion. The eschatological dimension at least adds a sense of urgency to some of the ethical teachings of Jesus (e.g., anger, lust). But there is also a content to the ethic of Jesus which is influenced by the presence and impending fulfillment of the reign of God. The ethical teaching of Jesus is a constant reminder of the absolute claim which the presence of the reign of God makes on the follower of Jesus. Jesus does not propose universal norms of conduct which are obliging for all Christians under all circumstances. Rather, in a very graphic way Jesus pictures man before the call of the reign of God's love. The reign of God places an all-engaging claim upon the hearer. Nothing else matters or counts when compared to the reign of God proclaimed and inaugurated by Jesus. Many of the ethical sayings of Jesus confront the individual with the inexorable claim of the presence of God's call. Jesus' graphic descriptions prescind from all other circumstances which might enter the picture. The neighbor in need and the follower of Jesus are placed face to face in a dramatic fashion.

The complexity of human problems is cast aside. Jesus prescinds from all other circumstances and conditions while showing the claim of the reign of God and the neighbor in need upon the individual follower. No mention is made of the binding obligations which a man might have to his wife or family. Jesus prescinds from all such realities and simply shows in a very stark and dramatic way the radical claim of the reign of God and the needs of the neighbor upon his followers. The Christian, like Jesus himself, should be willing to sacrifice all for others. One can understand better the sayings about turning the other cheek, walking the extra mile, giving to everyone who asks, imitating the lilies of the field, hating father and mother, plucking out an eye or cutting off a hand which would separate man from God, as illustrative of the radical demands of the presence of the reign of God.

The gift of the reign of God puts an unconditional claim on the believer. But what does such a simplistic view of reality mean for the follower of Jesus who lives amid the complexity of modern human existence? Very often the Christian is confronted by many people in need. The Christian has manifold responsibilities that are always on the horizon. Can a Christian so give himself and his time to the neighbor in need that he forgets his familial obligations? What value is the simplistic evangelical description of the dramatic confrontation between an individual and the call of the kingdom or the neighbor in need?

The radical and seemingly impossible ethical teaching of Jesus is more than rhetoric. Jesus indicates the goal and direction that should characterize the life and actions of his followers. "Give to everyone who asks" is an impossible ethical imperative, but such a demand indicates the constant thrust that characterizes the life of the Christian. I cannot claim everything I have as my own and dispose of it in any way I want. The Christian realizes that his talents, treasure, and abilities are in the service of the kingdom and the neighbor in need. There are times when the follower of Jesus might not be able to turn the other cheek; but the model of patience and forebearance, coupled with mercy and not vengeance, always remains meaningful. Occasionally the Christian might deem violence necessary to protect innocent human life (e.g., a young child being attacked by a demented person), but the thrust of the radical teaching of Jesus can never be forgotten.

Eschatological considerations introduce an inevitable tension into Christian ethics. The tension results from the fact that the reign of God in Christ is now present and is going forward toward its fullness. We are living in the times in between the two comings of Jesus. The reign of God is present but not yet fully present. The incipient presence of the eschaton calls for a continual growth and development. The followers of Jesus can never rest content with the present. The eschatological future is to some extent now present and urging the Christian forward. The true follower of the New Law can never say: "All these I have kept from my youth." The ethical teaching of Jesus calls for a continual effort to overcome the obstacles and shortcomings of the present moment.

DEFICIENCIES IN THE PAST

Unfortunately, the recent Catholic tradition has forgotten the eschatological tension both in the life of the individual and in the life of the Church. Theology did not insist upon the radical teachings of Jesus. In popular teaching the Christian ethical demands were reduced to a comparatively few, negative, universal norms which were to be observed by all. Such norms not only gave a negative tone to the Christian life, but comparatively easy norms of conduct robbed the Christian life of its inherent dynamism. The Christian could be content with having observed a comparatively few norms of morality. The Christian found a false sense of security in such norms and occasionally succumbed to a pharisaical attitude. On a wider scale the Church itself suffered from the same defect. The charge of triumphalism rang true in the

Conciliar halls of Vatican II. The Church forgot its pilgrim status and lost the dynamic thrust of continual growth and conversion. The radical ethical teaching of Jesus prevents either his Church or his followers from ever remaining content and smug in the present stage of life.

Specifically in the area of moral theology, Catholic teaching has tried to avoid the tension created by the ethics of Jesus. As a result Catholic theology very frequently has lost the eschatological dimension of growth; or, less frequently, has required of all a goal that was not always attainable. The loss of the dynamic thrust in moral theology can be seen in the teaching on the right to life. Catholic theologians have not been in the forefront of those who were arguing for the abolition of capital punishment, the suspension of nuclear testing, the cessation of war. Why not? Catholic teaching over the years developed a very intricate system or theory for dealing with problems of life and death. Direct killing of the innocent is never permitted; but the state has the right to kill malefactors, and individuals may kill others indirectly or in self-defense. However, such a norm, considered only in itself, lacks the dynamic thrust in favor of human life which should always characterize the Christian life. The principles governing the questions of life and death solve complex problems too easily. The follower of Jesus can never be content when forced to take a life. Every taking of life is a falling short of the radical ethic of Jesus. Perhaps at times it is necessary to take human life; but a Christian can take life with only the greatest remorse and reluctance.

Likewise in the question of war, theologians tend to dismiss too easily the deaths of thousands of people because they are only "indirect" killings. There may be times when the follower of Jesus must act according to the principles of indirect killing, but the Christian can never lose sight of the thrust imposed by the radical ethic of Jesus. Personally I cannot be a total pacifist in the sense that at times resorting to violence might be necessary to defend innocent people. However, the follower of Jesus always strives in the direction of pacifism. When killing is deemed necessary it can only be as a reluctant accommodation to the needs of the present time.

In many other areas Catholic theology has too easily accommodated itself to the present moment and forgotten the radical ethical demands of Jesus. Problems of slavery and race immediately come to mind. The Church and the theologians too easily acquiesced to predominant social patterns and structures. The Church cannot be altogether proud of its historical record on behalf of the freedom and dignity of man. Theologians and Church leaders have also been absent from leadership in the fight for the equality of women. The institutional Church seems to have perpetuated a system of colonization rather than fighting for the rights of people to govern themselves. In the ninth century Pope Nicholas I condemned physical constraint and torture; but a few centuries later the Church used torture and violence to further its own dubious goals. Papal teaching on justice and the rights of the working man is a comparatively bright chapter in the history of the Church. But history also reminds us that Karl Marx recognized the problem almost half a century before Leo XIII wrote his encyclicals.

The followers of Jesus and his Church can never forget the radical ethical teaching of the Master. However, the imperfections and sinfulness that characterize the present times will mean that the Christian often falls far short of the goal described by Jesus. Accommodation to the present reality is a necessity at times. But the absolute claim of the reign of God and the needs of our neighbor never allow the Christian to be content when it is necessary to fall short of the radical moral teaching of Jesus. The Christian always possesses an uneasy conscience. Compromise and adaptation to present needs can only be accepted reluctantly. Catholic theology has too often forgotten the uneasy conscience of the Christian in confronting the imperfect and sinful situations of the present time. Jesus calls his followers to be the light of the world and the salt of the earth.

IDEAL AND ACCOMMODATION

On the other side of the paradox, there are times when the universal norms in Catholic theology do not sufficiently take into consideration the reluctant but necessary possibility of not fully accomplishing the moral demand of Jesus. Perhaps the universal norm absolutizes what is a radical demand of Jesus which is not always achievable. The biblical teaching on divorce may be an example. (Naturally one cannot settle the teaching of the Catholic Church on divorce merely from biblical evidence, but the solution proposed according to the biblical understanding may very well be applicable to the present understanding of divorce in the Church.) In the Sermon on the Mount in Matthew the two verses on divorce follow the radical maxim of plucking out an eye or cutting off a hand if the eye or the hand lead one astray. The divorce passage is followed by the saying of Jesus that his true followers will never take any oaths but will be content to make their speech a plain "yes" or "no." In Matthew 19 the matter of divorce is approached in the context of the two opposing opinions existing among the rabbis. Jesus definitely upholds the indissolubility of marriage. Jesus explains the permission given by Moses in the Old Testament on the grounds of the hardness of the heart of the people. However, there is in Matt 19:9 the puzzling exception clause ("except for unchastity"—*porneia*) which also appears in Matt 5:32.

Within the New Testament times there are accommodations in the teaching of absolute indissolubility. The famous

Pauline privilege represents a falling short of the ideal proposed by Jesus. Paul, according to some exegetes, allowed converts to the faith to marry a new wife if their heathen wife wanted a separation (1 Cor 7: 12-16). Exegetes have developed many different theories for the famous incisions in the gospel of Matthew. Although scripture scholars disagree on the exact meaning of such exceptions, many would agree that the exceptions were probably added to the primitive statements by the early Church. The exceptions may well represent some type of accommodation within the early Church to the radical ethical demands of Jesus. The accommodations made in New Testament times, whatever they may have been, are not the only possible accommodations that the Church and Christians might have to make in the course of time.

The radical ethic of Jesus, although seemingly impossible, is relevant precisely because the presence of the reign of God tending toward its eschatological fulfillment places an absolute claim upon the follower of Jesus. Even when the Christian must fall short of the radical demand of Jesus, he cannot rest content with the accommodation to the needs and imperfections of present reality. The dangers in any ethic of pure accommodation are manifold. The collaboration of citizens with the war aims and activities of their governments is perhaps the most painful and obvious example for the modern Christian. The conscience of the Christian can never rest content with any type of accommodation, but always seeks new ways to pursue the direction and goal pointed out in the radical ethics of Jesus. The ethic of Jesus for the contemporary Christian involves a creative tension between the present and the final stage of the reign of God.

Unfortunately, man finds such tension difficult to live with. Some eliminate the tension by forgetting about the future and the continual call to growth and development. Others overthrow the tension by naively forgetting the present reality. Until very recently Catholic theology and life dissolved the tension and the frustration by forgetting about the radical ethics of Jesus and the consequent call for continual growth and even revolution. Absolute norms capable of being observed to the letter provided man with a false sense of security. Catholics acted as if they had all the answers to the problems confronting mankind. The certitude and the security of the Church were a rock against the shifting sands of human existence. Various types of security were built into the system in addition to the watered down ethical demands which gave a reassuring sense of security to those who obeyed them. Indulgences, First Fridays, and First Saturdays were all means of providing assurance of eternal salvation. The Church had all the answers to the problems that confronted man and his society. The Church itself did not know doubt, confusion, growth, pain, and tension.

Catholic life and theology in the post Vatican II era no longer claim to have the security and certitude that characterized Catholic life and teaching just a few short years ago. However, there is still a tendency to avoid the doubts, growing pains, and frustrations of a pilgrim people and a pilgrim Church. For Catholic life today the older securities and certitudes are gone forever; but many still look, somewhat naively, for a false sense of security. In opening up the Church to the world, in opening up ourselves to others, we reveal our own uncertainties, frustrations and weaknesses. In the midst of such frustration men easily seek a false sense of security. Postconciliar life in the Church has seen a number of new Messiahs appear on the horizon with great expectations, but the hopes of their followers are quickly dashed against the realities of human existence in the times in between. Many pinned their hopes on the liturgy in English or lately on an entirely new liturgy, but experience shows that the liturgy will never become the new Messiah.

Many other Messiahs have appeared—ranging from Martin Buber to Harvey Cox to the scriptural renewal. But the eschaton has not yet come. Perhaps the pessimism of Sartre serves as an excellent reminder to the naive personalism and optimism of many today.

Some Catholics have abandoned a triumphalism in the Church only to embrace a triumphalism of the world or the secular city. I firmly believe that the mission of the Christian and the Church is in service of the world, but the present state of the world is not entirely salvific. There is too much suffering and inequality in our own country, let alone in a world blighted by injustice, ignorance, and hunger, for the Christian to be content with the present situation. Professor Charles West of Princeton Theological Seminary, in describing the meeting on Church and Society sponsored by the World Council of Churches in Geneva in the summer of 1966, remarked about the opposition to the theological advocates of the secular city. West claims that the majority of theologians from the underdeveloped countries were "theological guerrillas" who saw revolution as the only way of shaking off the shackles of contemporary political and social structures. The "theological technocrats" of the secular city were amazed at the vehemence of the revolutionaries.

To live with the eschatological tension is difficult. The Christian too experiences doubt, frustration, opposition, and resistance to any growth. One who realizes the difficulties in breaking away from his own selfishness and sinfulness also understands the slowness of growth in the structures of human existence. To become resigned to the present is just as inadequate a solution as to expect miraculous progress without opposition or frustration. For the Christian the virtue of hope allows him to live the eschatological tension. Hope constantly beckons in the direction of the final stage of the kingdom of God. The follower of Jesus can never rest content with the present situation of his own change of heart or the present situation of humanity. But hope also strengthens the follower of Jesus against the frustrations and opposition that accompany any growth. Hope makes the Paschal Mystery of Christ a reality. Only by dying does the Christian rise in the newness of life.

Despair looms all too easily on the horizon for one who expects the eschaton to come too easily or too quickly. The greatness of God's gift to man is the fact that man has his role to play in bringing about the new heaven and the new earth. The radical ethic of Jesus could very easily bring one to despair because of the impossibility that it entails. However, the ethic of Jesus is both gift and demand. Man's inability to live according to the strenuous moral teaching of Jesus is a constant reminder of his need for God's mercy and forgiveness. At the same time the radical ethical demand serves as a constant reminder to the Christian to open himself ever more to the call of God and neighbor. The Christian creatively tries to make himself and his world. All the old securities and certitudes are gone. There are no false props that the Christian can use. Christian maturity demands that the follower of Jesus stand on his own feet and carve out his human existence despite all the frustrations and doubts of life. The Christian as a pilgrim traveling to the new heaven and the new earth never has the luxury and the security of one who has already arrived at his final destination. In the insecurity of the journey only his hope in the Word and Work of God gives him the courage to continue. Hope is the virtue that allows the Christian to live the tension of the reign of God present but not yet fully here.

There are tendencies in the evangelical ethic to abandon entirely the life of man in this world. However, the contemporary Christian realizes that the needs of his neighbor can and must be met at the present time. The Christian's hope in the final coming of the reign of God does not furnish him with any blueprint for human development and growth. Only a naive biblicism would expect to find in the scriptures the solutions to the problems confronting man and society today. The ethical teaching of Jesus urges his followers to creatively find solutions to come to the aid of the neighbor in need.

Like the individual Christian, the Church too must take seriously the moral teaching of Jesus and the virtue of hope. The primary concern of the Church should be the neighbor in need. The Church constantly needs to rethink the ways in which it tries to accomplish its primary purposes. The tendency to seek security in the means that were helpful in the past is all too tempting. There is also the temptation to seek security in other things and not in the Word of God in Christ. For a long time the Church tried to find its security in the protection of the State. Now the temptation seems to be for the Church to find its security in brick and mortar institutions. Structures and institutions will always be necessary, but they only serve to help the Church be faithful to the mission and teaching of Jesus which puts primary emphasis on the neighbor in need. The Church should not seek false security in status, wealth or power. The pilgrim Church finds its only security in the promise of its founder.

The relevancy of the gospel ethic of Jesus is the challenge and vocation given to the followers of Jesus and his Church.

Bibliography for Chapter 1

W. D. Davies, *The Sermon on the Mount* (Cambridge University Press, 1966). Davies answers both yes and no, with more emphasis on the yes, to the question: Has Matthew departed from the mind of Jesus by making the words of Jesus in the Sermon on the Mount into "the new law"?

C. H. Dodd, *Gospel and Law* (Cambridge University Press, 1951). Four essays originally given as the Bampton Lectures at Columbia University in 1950. The radical ethical sayings of Jesus are interpreted in the third essay as showing the goal and direction toward which the Christian strives and also serving as a reminder of man's constant need for forgiveness.

Bernard Häring C.SS.R., "The Normative Value of the Sermon on the Mount," *The Catholic Biblical Quarterly*, 29 (July 1967), 365-385. The article merely summarizes the main points in the already existing literature. Häring argues that the saving message and the moral imperative are one and that the ethical sayings of the Sermon are "goal commandments."

John Knox, *The Ethic of Jesus in the Teaching of the Church* (Abingdon Press, 1961). A somewhat popular and very readable summary of the different solutions to the problem of the radical ethic of Jesus.

Noël Lazure, O.M.I., *Les Valeurs Morales de la Théologie Johannique* (J. Gabalda, 1965). The latest and one of the few studies devoted exclusively to the moral teaching of John.

Norman Perrin, *The Kingdom of God in the Teaching of Jesus* (Westminster Press, 1963). A fine, scholarly summary of the discussion about the nature of the kingdom and its relationship to ethics from Schleiermacher to the present.

Paul Ramsey, *Basic Christian Ethics* (Charles Scribner's Sons, 1950). A text in Christian ethics with a long introductory section on the love ethic of Jesus. However, the later works of Ramsey show, at least, a different emphasis in his moral methodology.

Rudolf Schnackenburg, *The Moral Teaching of the New Testament* (Herder and Herder, 1964). A one volume summary and synthesis of the moral teaching of the entire New Testament.

Ceslaus Spicq O.P., *Agape in the New Testament,* 3 vols. (B. Herder, 1963, 1965, 1966). An exegetical and scriptural study of agape in the New Testament without the very complete footnotes found in the original French volume.

Ceslaus Spicq O.P., *Théologie Morale du Nouveau Testament,* 2 vols. (J. Gabalda, Paris, 1965). A comparatively complete and analytical treatment (there is no attempt made at a synthesis of the teaching) of the different moral themes and teachings in the New Testament. The footnotes with very complete bibliographies are most valuable.

Conversion: The Central Moral Message of Jesus

Chapter Two

Conversion is the central moral message of Jesus. St. Mark summarizes the entire teaching and preaching of Jesus in terms of the call to conversion. Jesus came into Galilee preaching the good news of the reign of God: "The time has come . . . and the reign of God is at hand. Be converted and believe in the good news" (Mark 1:15).

This chapter will develop three points. First, the call to conversion is the joyful proclamation of God's love calling for a change of heart in the individual. The second point will consider God's role in the work of conversion, whereas the third point will discuss man's response in the process of conversion. From the different theoretical aspects of the teaching on conversion practical conclusions will be drawn for Christian life in our times and for the sacrament of penance which is the sacrament of conversion.

I. CONVERSION AS THE JOYFUL
CHANGE OF HEART

Jesus is direct, straightforward, simple; and yet Christian teaching and preaching today is too often legalistic in tone. People are warned to do this, to avoid that. The emphasis falls on a particular action or mode of external conduct. The authentic Christian message, however, calls above all for a change of heart—a radical, internal change of the person; external actions will follow from the person's changed heart. The gospel reminds us that the good tree will bring forth good fruit and the evil tree will bring forth evil fruit (Matt 7:17-20). The Christian message aims to produce the good tree from which comes good fruit. If a man changes his heart, then his actions will change accordingly.

The Greek word used in the Septuagint Bible for conversion is *epistrephein*. In secular literature the word meant "to turn toward"; frequently it referred to the person who turned himself toward an object, or just turned himself around. In time, the word acquired a metaphorical and moral usage. One common meaning was to turn attention toward a particular object or person. The Greek word for conversion also came to signify a change, a transformation in the way of thinking and acting.

Epistrephein is employed in the Greek scriptures for the Hebrew word *shuv*. *Shuv* adds another dimension to the meaning of conversion: the notion of coming back or returning. The Hebrew word recalls the many times in the history of salvation when the people of Israel abandoned their alliance with Yahweh and worshiped false gods. Yahweh, however, was faithful always to his covenant; he continued to call his people back to the alliance. The New Testament frequently joins together the words for conversion and repentance (*metanoia*). The two words connote the change that occurs in the person who hears the good news of salvation and responds to it. Consequently, conversion came to mean a profound transformation of the whole person.

New Testament theology teaches that conversion is the joyful change of heart that comes from hearing the good news of salvation. The good news is that God, here and now, offers his love to man. The motive for conversion is the presence of the reign of God in Christ. Translations frequently employ the word *kingdom*, but *reign* perhaps better approaches the meaning of scripture. *Kingdom* tends to connote a static reality and is too often identified with a monarchical political structure. *Reign* avoids the prejorative connotations of *kingdom* and better shows the reality of the reign of God as his love made manifest to man, especially in the person of Jesus. To be converted and believe in the good news, then, means to change your heart and to accept the gift of God in Christ Jesus. This change of heart is not, however, a moment or a static state once and forever effected. Conversion is a continuous turning, a growing, a becoming. And if it is not that, then it is the opposite—a turning away from God.

The *kerygma*, or central preaching of the early Church, tries to bring about a change of heart by recalling the marvelous works that God has done for man, especially in the resurrection of Jesus. Through his resurrection Jesus has become Lord—Messiah—and eternal priest. The proper response of the hearer is conversion and baptism in the name of Jesus. The Acts of the Apostles contains many examples of calls to conversion as preached by the first disciples of Christ. The theme is constant: the good news of salvation requires a change of heart in the person who, hearing, believes.

The parable of the Prodigal Son (Luke 15:11-32), perhaps, contains the most appealing scriptural presentation of the meaning of conversion. (Some scriptural exegetes prefer to call the parable the story of the merciful Father, for the essential features of the parable stress the prodigal—lavish—mercy and forgiveness of our Father in heaven.) The son demands his inheritance and leaves his father's house to go to a far away country. There appears to be no good reason for his leaving but to be free from the parental yoke and to pursue pleasure. The delusion of sin quickly becomes evident. The son does not find what he expected. Instead of happiness, freedom and joy, he experiences only sorrow, slavery and misery.

The details of the story bring out the miserable condition of the sinner, the degradation of sin. Sin is not just a wrong action; sin is not primarily the breaking of a law. The parable poignantly portrays sin as the breaking of the intimate relationship of love with the Father. The sinner leaves the loving abundance of the Father's house to seek his happiness elsewhere.

What is the conversion of the foolish son? Conversion means the joyful return to the Father. The son has experienced his own misery and realized his error in leaving the house of his father. The return to the father's house is a joyful experience. The father does not treat his son harshly; there are no words or scenes. The father does not even remonstrate with his wayward son. Rather, the father runs to greet him and cries tears of joy because his lost son has been found. A joyful banquet celebrates the return of the son.

The parable of the Merciful Father portrays the meaning of sin and conversion. The early Church used the parable to refer to those Christians who had deserted Christ (obviously Christ could never have used the parable in that sense) but were called to experience the joyful return to the Church, the house of the Father. For the Christian who has broken his relationship of love with God through sin, the call to conversion echoes the story of the Merciful Father who is ready and waiting to receive his wayward sons with outstretched arms and a joyful celebration.

Other New Testament themes reinforce the understanding of conversion as the joyful change of heart. The basic moral imperative of the Christian life is love of God and neighbor; but love presupposes that change of heart which has taken place in the Christian. The prophet Jeremiah had looked forward to the messianic era when God would give a new heart to his people (Jeremiah 31:33). The old law was written on stone tablets in the form of a code, but the new law is engraved in the heart of the Christian. The new law is the love of God and neighbor. The selfish and stoney heart of man would be replaced by a heart of love.

St. Paul develops the notion of the law of the Spirit as superior to the codified law given to Moses. The Spirit is the one who gives life. The most common attribute of the Spirit in the creeds of the early Church was the "life-giving" Spirit. The Spirit is the source of life for the Christian. The Spirit is the love of God present in our hearts; he is the guiding force in the moral life of the Christian. The primary law for the Christian is not any external code or list of rules, but rather the life-giving Spirit who dwells in the hearts of the just. Conversion means that man now receives the great gift of the Spirit. In other words, the reception of the Spirit demands the change of heart (the new life) described in conversion.

Sacramental theology teaches that baptism and penance are the sacraments of conversion. Through baptism the Christian receives new life in the Spirit. In baptism the Christian shares in the Paschal Mystery of Christ, passing over from death to life. The symbolism of the sacrament, whereby we become children of the Father, shows the great change that baptism brings to the new Christian. Penance, in turn, is the sacrament of conversion for those Christians who have broken their relationship of love with God. Both sacraments of conversion illustrate the meaning of conversion as the change of heart.

PRACTICAL CONCLUSIONS

The central notion of conversion as the joyful change of heart entails many practical consequences for those who try to teach and live the Christian life. First, the call to conversion always should echo the joyful call of Christ. Conversion is man's response to the good news of God's love—the gospel. The urgency of the call to conversion in the New Testament stems not from motives of fear but from the greatness of the gift of God and the shortness of time. Now is the great moment of history. In a sense, the countdown of all history has been leading to the coming of Jesus. Now he is here. Now is the opportunity for man to accept the great gift of God. There is no time to delay. Leave everything—father, mother, brothers, sisters—to follow the call of Christ (Luke 14:26-33).

The New Testament call to conversion differs somewhat from the call to conversion addressed to the Israelites in the Old Testament. In the Old Testament conversion frequently was motivated by fear of punishments that would be inflicted if conversion did not take place. Christian teaching and preaching has tended, unfortunately, to overemphasize this motivation of fear and punishment. The New Testament motive for conversion is always the good news of God's love made present for his people.

Popular teaching not only has overemphasized the importance of punishment but also has distorted the meaning of punishment in Christian life. Theologians today tend to see punishment as the natural conseqence of sin, the refusal of God's love. Punishment is primarily intrinsic and not extrinsic; that is, punishment is the logical consequence of the action performed. God is never the author of punishment. God works only to save. Man punishes himself. Punishment is not just an arbitrary threat to deter a person from a particular action. In Genesis, death is the punishment for sin. But death for sin is not an arbitrary punishment, as would be the threat to a child of no TV if he misbehaves. Since sin involves separation from God, the author of life, death is intimately connected with sin as its necessary consequence and its ultimate goal. Heaven and hell are not primarily rewards and punishments; rather, they designate the logical consequence of the Christian's life in this world. Reward and punishment themes have been exaggerated in Christian teaching—perhaps because they have been seen as only extrinsic to the reality itself. The primary motivation for conversion remains God's love and not the threat of punishment.

A second practical consequence of conversion as the joyful change of heart concerns the sacrament of penance. The Constitution on the Liturgy has pointed out the need for a change in the ritual of the sacrament of penance. One of the greatest deficiencies of the present ritual is its failure to accent conversion, the joy of return and reconciliation with the heavenly Father. Yet even in the present rite, the confessor can do much to renew the meaning of penance as the joyful return to the house of the Father. When dealing with a frightened penitent, away from the sacrament for a long time, the confessor can begin with a short explanation of the parable of the Merciful Father. The story can illustrate to the penitent the experience of joyful reunion with his loving Father. In penance the Father lovingly embraces his wayward son and celebrates his return home.

An overly juridicial approach has colored, even camouflaged, the true meaning of the sacrament of penance. The primary role of the confessor is to proclaim the good news of conversion and to celebrate the joyful reconciliation of the wayward son to the Father. The confessor is above all the herald of God's loving mercy and the representative of the community in the joy of reconciliation with a wayward member of the community. From a practical viewpoint today, the confessor realizes the impossibility of judging the sins of others. Moral theology textbooks only taught him to distinguish the objective species of sin. The problem generally concerns the subjective state of the person. Very often the confessor cannot judge adequately or with certainty whether or not the penitent has broken his relationship of love with God. Both theory and practice should show that the primary role of the confessor is not that of judge. Theologians must explore just what the Council of Trent meant in talking about the judgment in the sacrament of penance. The judgment of God present in the sacrament of penance is the merciful judgment of the saving God. The justice of God administered in the sacrament of penance is not the justice of a court of law but the justice by which God mercifully makes us aware that once more we share, through Christ's death and resurrection, a new life with God. The judgment of God as found in the sacrament of penance is not the judgment of the confessor about the disposition or worthiness of the penitent but rather the proclamation or saving judgment pronounced in the name of the Church—"I absolve you."

A third practical consequence for Christian life also follows from the notion of conversion as the joyful change of heart. Too often in the past Catholic teaching has insisted on particular, individual actions in and of themselves. External conformity received the foremost emphasis. However, the primary aim of Christian teaching is to change the heart of the hearer. Again, the circumstances of our own age reinforce the need for Christian teaching to center primarily on the change of heart and not on external actions as such. In the complexity of modern living, Christianity demands much more than just conformity to a comparatively few norms of conduct. Christian education should aim at forming the new heart through which the Christian can sensitively respond to the call of God and neighbor in the intricate situations of modern life. Actions spring from the heart; hence, the heart first must be renewed. Catechists, preachers and parents cannot be content to teach mere conformity to a few external norms. Rather, education aims at forming a mature person who can respond to his own conscience in making necessary decisions in the complicated reality of life. One can never forget that external actions are important; good intentions alone will never suffice for the Christian working to build the new heaven and the new earth. However, the primary intent of our teaching must be to change the hearts of men.

Conversion is the change of heart by which a person becomes a friend of God and a recipient of his love. Mortal sin is the opposite of conversion. Mortal sin is the change of heart by which a person turns away from his relationship of love with God. Mortal sin marks the refusal of life, the refusal of light, the refusal of Christ. Sin, like conversion, involves a profound change of heart. Although theology has taught always that sin is a turning away from God, popular teaching too often has identified sin with a particular, individual, external action. We say that lying is a sin, or we ask if war is a sin. The action, however, becomes sinful only if the action involves a change of heart. The external act alone can never express with certitude the fact that the person has had a change of heart. The wrong action might be the sign of ignorance or passion or an honest mistake—or a change of heart. Every wrong action does not involve necessarily a change of heart. Theology and catechetics should carefully distinguish between wrong actions and sin.

Modern psychology underlines the impossibility of knowing the heart of a man from any one external action. Scripture seems to indicate the same. In the judgment scene portrayed in Matthew's gospel (25:31-46), man's relationship with God is known and manifested through the totality of his relationships with his fellowmen. To know if a person is a friend of God, we should consider the way he acts toward others. "When I was hungry, when I was thirsty, when I was naked, when I was in prison. . . ." Common sense reminds us also of the impossibility of judging a person just on the basis of one meeting or one action. Since mortal sin involves a profound change of heart, it cannot be identified with an external act merely considered in itself. The external action is grossly sinful only to the extent that it is the expression of the fundamental change of heart which is sin.

The realization that conversion and sin involve a change of heart again has important consequences for the sacrament of penance. Penance is not a "magical" rite. Penance does not merely cancel out a few bad actions or "wipe away" some mortal sins. The sacrament of penance calls for a profound change of heart that involves the core of human existence. The so-called "devotional confession" or "confession of venial sins" involves a strengthening of the new heart of the Christian. The actions required of the Christian illustrate the profound change which penance brings about. The penitent Christian now is willing to love and forgive others in the same way that Jesus has loved and forgiven him. This is the central biblical message of conversion. It has to have important consequences for the teaching and living of the Christian life.

II. CONVERSION AND THE REIGN OF GOD
AS HIS GIFT

Conversion to the reign of God in Christ is the central moral message of the New Testament. However, conversion and the reign of God are primarily God's work and not ours. The primary truth of Christianity is the fact that God saves us. Too often Catholic theology and catechetics have emphasized the role of man in salvation. Too often people think that man saves himself by his own actions. Salvation is frequently pictured as an agreement between God and man. If man does these things and fulfills these conditions, then God will give him the reward of salvation. Theology has always tried to wrestle with the God-man relationship, but a danger of emphasizing the role of one at the expense of the other is always present. Ultimately, the work of theology is to explain the relative roles of God and man, faith and works, gospel and law. Both aspects are essential. In the past, Roman Catholic theology has not always stressed the primacy of God's love. In many ways the scriptures recall the primary truth of Christianity—it is God who saves. God in Christ works the transformation and brings man from darkness to light, from death to life, from slavery to the freedom of the children of God.

The scriptures show that salvation is primarily God's gift by the emphasis on the privileged members of the reign of God. One might naturally expect that the privileged members of the reign of God would be the rich, the powerful, and the influential. But according to the scriptures the privileged members of the reign of God are the poor, children, and sinners. The privileged position of the poor, children, and sinners indicates that man does nothing to deserve or earn the gift of salvation. The non-value of the recipients of the gift of God shows the divine good pleasure in loving man and establishing his reign. This insistence on the poor, sinners, and children also illustrates the necessary disposition on the part of men who are to receive the gift of God's love.

The poor occupy a special place in the scriptures. The fact that the poor have the good news preached to them is one of the great signs of the presence of the messianic and eschatological era. The spirituality of the poor, the *ᶜanawim Yahweh*, permeates the scriptures. In the Old Testament there was a gradual development in the understanding of wealth and poverty. Originally, wealth was looked upon as a sign of divine favor and blessing. Even the promise to the people of the covenant was in terms of land and posterity—aspects frequently associated with wealth. Social legislation in Israel was based on the notion that wealth is a blessing from God. No one of the people of Israel should be poor; hence legislation was introduced to help the poor in the Old Testament. Meanwhile, the Hebrew word *ᶜani*, meaning to be stooped or bent over, was used not only for the poor but also to describe the necessary disposition of the Israelite before his God. Humility characterized the attitude of man before the God of the covenant. A more mature reflection brought about the realization that wealth is not always a sign of God's blessing and poverty does not always indicate sin. The nation of Israel itself experienced suffering and privation through the exile. Israel believed they were the chosen people of God, but they now underwent exile and humiliation before their neighbors. Existentially, material poverty became associated with poverty of spirit or humility. The *ᶜanawim* were the true clients of Yahweh. Their physical privation, exile, and poverty only made them more conscious of their true dependence on Yahweh. They could look only to him for deliverance and salvation. Hope and waiting thus characterized the people of God in the Old Testament.

They were waiting for the eschatological coming of the messianic era. They lived in the hope of the coming. Salvation was not to be found in horses or chariots or gold or silver but only in trustful hope in deliverance by Yahweh.

Jeremiah is an excellent example of the spirituality of the poor of Yahweh. Jeremiah had received his mission from Yahweh. However, he experienced great suffering, privation, and frustration. At times he cried out in despair and cursed the day he was born. But through his poverty and suffering he learned that he lived in total dependence on Yahweh. The mysterious suffering servant of Isaiah is also a type of the *ᶜanawim*. Poverty and suffering would make him too realize the more his dependence on Yahweh. The poor of Yahweh live in total hope and dependence on Yahweh. Poverty makes them more conscious of this. Thus the poor were the special clients of Yahweh and the spirituality of the *ᶜanawim* characterizes the people of the covenant. Such a spirituality constantly points to salvation and deliverance as the gift from God. Man's hope is not based on anything else. As a poor man, he has nothing else. However, despite all his sufferings and frustrations the poor man retains his hope in Yahweh. The story of Yahweh's dealing with his people is the lesson of placing their trust and confidence in his saving power and in no other person or thing. The poor man really has nothing in which he can trust or glory. His hands are always outstretched to receive from others. The poor man realizes that whatever he does have is a gift from another.

The privileged position of the sinner in the reign of God also illustrates the fundamental truth that salvation is primarily God's gift to man. Obviously, the sinner has nothing to offer God in return for his love. The sinner has no claim whatsoever on the love and the mercy of God. The privileged position of the sinner merely highlights the divine mercy and forgiveness. At first glance, the sinner would seem to be the person furthest from the reign of God. How can one ever dare to say that the sinner has a privileged position in the reign of God? The goodness and mercy of God know no bounds. There is no better illustration than the privileged position of the sinner to show that salvation depends primarily on God's loving mercy and forgiveness. Man does nothing to earn salvation. His good works or merits do not count. The determining factor is the love of God, who allows his sun to shine on the just and the unjust and extends his mercy to all men.

The privilege of children also emphasizes that salvation is God's gift to man. The child is the perennial symbol of helplessness. The child has nothing to offer but needs the love and protection of others. Luke the evangelist puts on the lips of Jesus a prayer thanking his Father who has chosen to reveal these things to the little ones: "Yes, Father, for such was thy good pleasure" (Luke 10:22). God has revealed his love and his works to man not because of man's actions or merits, but simply because of his own benevolence, because of his own good pleasure. Salvation, conversion, the reign of God, is his gift to man. The privileged position of the child merely highlights the gratuitousness of God's reign.

The New Testament scriptures tell us of the saving work of God in Christ. The good news is precisely the gracious love of God for man. Some sections of the scriptures which seem furthest from an announcement of the good news are in reality an announcement of the saving love of God. The beatitudes furnish an excellent example. The New Testament knows two different versions of the beatitudes in the synoptic gospels of Matthew and Luke. The two versions take a slightly different approach. Luke has just four beatitudes and four corresponding woes or maledictions. Even more significantly, Luke twice presents a temporal antithesis —now and then. "Blessed are you who hunger now, for you shall be satisfied! Blessed are you who weep now, for you shall laugh. . . . But woe to you rich! for you are now having your comfort. . . . Woe to you who laugh now! for you shall mourn and weep" (Luke 6:21-26). The beatitudes are basically a proclamation of blessings and happiness. By his temporal antithesis Luke contrasts the unhappy lot of his hearers now with the happiness which will be theirs in the future. Future happiness is not seen as a reward but rather as the antithesis of the present situation. Luke's viewpoint is sapiential. Those who are sad now will be happy in the future. Their present condition of unhappiness shows that they have opted for happiness in the future. The future will be the inverse of the present situation.

Matthew uses the beatitudes in a different way. There are three characteristics peculiar to Matthew's use of them. Matthew has a total of eight or nine beatitudes rather than the four of Luke. In two places he introduces the word "justice" ("Blessed are they who hunger and thirst for justice. . . . Blessed are they who suffer persecution for justice's sake. . . ."). Also Matthew spiritualizes the beatitudes so that the poor become the poor in spirit. The additional beatitudes in Matthew which differ from Luke's version also emphasize dispositions and attitudes rather than concrete reality as in Luke. The word "justice" assumes a great importance in Matthew's gospel, even though it is seldom used in the other synoptic accounts. Justice describes the righteousness or the Christian ideal which should be incorporated in the life of the Christian. (Cf. the use of the term justice—*dikaiosune*—in Matt 5:20 and 6:1 as well as 3:15, 6:33, 21:32.) The Sermon on the Mount in Matthew is structured around the key sentences of Matthew 5:20 ("For I say to you that unless your justice exceeds that of the Scribes and Pharisees, you shall not enter the kingdom of heaven") and 6:1 ("Take heed not to do your good—*dikaiosune*—before men, in order

to be seen by them"). The Sermon on the Mount expounds
the justice and righteousness which should characterize the
life of the Christian. The Sermon in Matthew points out how
the follower of Jesus should live. The Sermon on the Mount
provides the setting in which Matthew collects the various
sayings that constitute the new law for the follower of Jesus.
Matthew thus employs the beatitudes within that same context. The Matthean beatitudes describe the attitudes and
dispositions which must characterize the life of the Christian.
Matthew uses the beatitudes in a catechetical and moralizing
way to point out how the Christian should live and thus be
happy.

Jacques Dupont maintains that both versions of the beatitudes differ from the more primitive version.[1] By an application of scientific exegetical tools, Dupont concludes the
primitive form contained only four beatitudes. But, more
important, the primitive meaning of the beatitudes differs
both from Luke and Matthew. The primitive form is a messianic proclamation of the good news of salvation. Blessings
and happiness are now proclaimed precisely because the messianic era has arrived. God's gift of salvation has finally come
—hence the reason for happiness. Dupont sees the primitive
form of the Beatitudes in line with other messianic procla-
mations; for example, the passage put on the lips of Jesus in
the synagogue at Nazareth (Luke 4:14-32). Jesus read the
section from Isaiah (Is 61) which describes the proclaiming
of the good news to the poor as a sign of the messianic era.
Jesus is then reported to claim that the text has been fulfilled
by him. Thus in the more primitive form the beatitudes
were a messianic and Christological proclamation of the
good news of salvation.

Matthew and Luke definitely changed the teaching of the
primitive form of the beatitudes according to their own purposes. Later redactions show the need to interpret the beati-

tudes in the setting of the early Church. The end of the world did not come as quickly as some may have expected. What meaning was there in the happiness and blessedness proclaimed in the beatitudes? Luke promised a future happiness which was contrasted with their existing poverty and unhappiness. Matthew used the beatitudes as a catechetical device to teach what was required in the daily life of the followers of Jesus. The blessed and happy are those who live according to the Sermon on the Mount. Notice the freedom with which the early evangelists interpreted the primitive form of the beatitudes. Thus in the different uses of the beatitudes one can find the necessary connection between gospel and law. The good news of salvation and man's response are joined together. However, for our present purposes, it is sufficient to point out that the primitive form of the beatitudes is a messianic proclamation of the gift of salvation now present. Even the beatitudes illustrate the primacy of God's loving concern in the salvation of man.

The parables of mercy in the gospel accounts are a third generic way in which the scriptures inculcate the fact that salvation is primarily God's loving gift. The parable of the Merciful Father (Luke 15) has already been mentioned as providing excellent illustrations both of sin as the breaking of a relationship of love and of conversion as the joyful return to the house of the father. Perhaps the story of the merciful Father makes an even greater impression if one sees the story in modern dress. After his parents have raised and educated him, a son abruptly takes all that he has and leaves home. The parents never hear from him again. Years later the son returns—poor, in debt, and in need of help. What might a modern father say to that son? Perhaps it would go something like this: "You really hurt your mother and me by going away. We were growing older, and I wanted you to stay and help with the business. Now that you have spent

all our hard-earned money and are miserable, you want us
to bail you out and welcome you again into our home. I am
afraid that it would not be fair for us to bring you back into
our home. It would not be fair to your brother who has spent
these many years working in my business and looking after
your mother and me. And really it would not be fair to you.
You have to prove yourself before we can take you back. This
might sound hard-hearted to you, but it will be the best
thing for you in the long run. You will be grateful in the
future for what I am doing for you because it will make a
man out of you." [2]

How different is the attitude of the merciful Father! He
does not demand any proof on our part. God's love is such a
gift that man could never do anything to prove worthy of
receiving it. Our worthiness or merits do not influence the
attitude of the merciful Father.

Meditate for a moment on the attitude of the elder brother
in the parable. When the elder brother discovered what occurred, he was angry and would not participate in the joyful
celebration of his brother's homecoming. The elder son re-
buked his father. The older son had served his father for
many years and obeyed all his commands, but his father had
never celebrated a feast for him. The action of the father is
not fair or just. The younger son who left home and spent
all his money on harlots and false friends now receives a
joyful reception and a banquet in his honor. Notice that the
elder son cannot even refer to the prodigal as "my brother"
but rather speaks of "your son." The attitude of the elder
son is typical of so many Christians who think only in terms
of justice and obedience and commandments. The elder son
cannot understand mercy and love and forgiveness. One
who knows only justice does not know the real meaning of
God's love and mercy.

The gospel narratives frequently teach that the first shall
be last and the last first (e.g., Matt 19:20; Mark 10:31, Luke

13:30). The parable of the laborers in the vineyard dramatically illustrates that man's approach is not the same as God's (Matt 20:1-16). Salvation is not primarily a recompense due in justice for the actions man has performed. The householder went out at various times in the day and brought in men to work in his vineyard. Some had begun work early in the morning, whereas others were hired late in the afternoon. At the end of the day, all were paid the same amount. However, those who had worked for the whole day and bore the brunt of the day's heat murmured against their employer. "It is not fair to give those who have worked but one hour in the cool of the evening the same wage given to us who have been working all day." At first sight, the complaint seems legitimate. The owner replies that he has done them no injustice. As owner he can choose to give to the latecomers the same wage given to the others. The owner defends his own freedom and generosity. The owner of the vineyard serves as a constant reminder that God is free in distributing his love as he wills. No one has any claim in justice on God's generosity. The parables of mercy repeat in a dramatic way the primary teaching of Christianity—it is God who saves.

PRACTICAL CONCLUSIONS

The emphasis on the primacy of God's love shows the importance of worship in the life of the Christian. Man is always a worshiper before God's loving gift. With grateful and reverent attitude men received everything from their God. The eucharistic motive in the Christian life is summarized in the prayer of the psalmist: "What shall I return to the Lord for all that he has done for me." The liturgical renewal in the Roman Catholic Church will achieve its fullest meaning only when men realize that their whole life is a eucharist—a continual and grateful response to the call of God. The entire life of the Christian manifests the gift and goodness of God's love. Our every action is in praise of God's loving mercy.

Worship is concentrated above all in liturgical celebrations. Catholic theology has maintained that the sacraments are signs of worship. However, the worship aspect of the sacrament of penance has been forgotten over the years. American Catholics frequently refer to the sacrament of penance as confession. Confession generally is understood as the revelation of one's sins. Contemporary society produces a great quantity of confession-type literature—the confessions of a Hollywood starlet or a teenage drug addict. However, the root meaning of the word confession (and the Latin *confiteri*) is not the revelation of sins or secrets. The *Confessions* of St. Augustine, for example, is not a revelation of the sins of his youth. "Confess" means to give thanks, to give praise. The psalmist gives thanks to the Lord (*confitemini Domino*) for he is good. Confession is primarily a giving thanks to God for his mercy and forgiveness. Nowhere is the mercy and forgiveness of God more evident than in the sacramental rite of penance. The penitent sinner experiences the meaning of the merciful love of God. The primary response of the penitent is worship—praise and thanksgiving to God in Christ for the great gift of forgiveness. Catholic theology of the sacrament of penance has neglected the primary meaning of confession.

A second practical conclusion from the reign of God as his gift concerns the place of justice in the God-man relationship. Too often Catholic theology has seen the God-man relationship exclusively in terms of justice and rewards. But the divine love does not depend on the works and dispositions of man. Justice, or *quid pro quo*, does not adequately explain the relationship between God and man. Some Catholics have opposed any change in the teaching on contraception or divorce on the grounds that any change would be unfair to the people who lived according to the present norms. Such people think they have earned their salvation by obeying these difficult norms and that others must do the same thing. The person who thinks in terms of justice frequently is very narrow and lacks the openness of heart which can understand mercy and forgiveness. The example of the elder son in the parable of the prodigal son could apply to many people today.

An overly exclusive emphasis on man's actions has produced a Pelagian mentality. Man forgets that everything he has comes as a gift from God and tends to think that he saves himself by his own works. Such an attitude easily leads to pharisaism. The pharisaical attitude describes the smug and content approach of those who believe they are justified by their own works. My observance of the law or my good works do not mean that I can look down my nose at others. The temptation to pharisaism is frequently pressing when the primacy of God's love and mercy is forgotten. Pharisaism implies a self-sufficiency and self-righteousness which is incompatible with the notion of the Christian as the poor of Yahweh who is constantly extending his hands to receive the gift of God's love. Emphasis on the primacy of God's love precludes the possibility of falling into the temptation of pharisaism.

Pelagian and pharisaical attitudes tend to forget the fullness of the ethical demand of Jesus. The ethical teaching of Jesus becomes watered down to a few norms which are somewhat easy to observe. By observing these norms men create the impression that they save themselves. Jesus condemned the Pharisees of old because they paid tithes even on the weeds in their gardens but forgot the weightier matters of the law—justice, mercy, and forgiveness. It is much easier to obey a few rubrics and man-made laws than it is to obey the fullness of the ethical teaching of Jesus. The follower of Jesus meditating on the radical demands of Jesus realizes that he can never fully observe the moral teaching of Jesus. The seemingly impossible demands of Jesus are a constant check to pharisaism, since no man can ever boast that he has observed all these things from his youth. Jesus' ethical teaching brings the Christian to the realization that he constantly falls short and is constantly in need of the saving love and mercy of God. The true follower of Jesus can never be smug or content, for his conscience reminds him how far short he falls of the imitation of the Master. The pharisaical approach loses the dynamic aspect of Christian life. The moral teaching of Jesus becomes watered down so that all men can observe it somewhat easily. Morality thus assumes a static and closed character rather than a dynamic and open approach.

An overemphasis on man's actions also leads to seeking a false sense of security. Man believes that his good actions give him the security of God's love. However, the hope of the Christian rests only in God's mercy and in nothing else. Too often Christians try to find security in created, human things; when in reality our only security comes from faith and trust in God. Also an exclusive emphasis on man's actions and the need to find security in such actions provide a fertile breeding ground for scrupulosity. The scrupulous person is overly concerned about his own actions precisely because these actions are absolutely important and essential for his salvation and security. The Christian who is primarily a worshiper with outstretched arms does not need to find his security in his own actions. The security for the follower of Jesus lies in our hope in his mercy and love. By forgetting the primacy of God's love in the work of conversion and the reign of God, one can easily distort the full meaning of the Christian message.

III. CONVERSION AND THE REIGN OF
GOD AS MAN'S RESPONSE

Christian theology has always known the tension between the role of God and the response of man in salvation. Too often in the past, debate has become sterile because the opposite sides really were not listening to one another. The present chapter does not intend to solve the theoretical problem of the respective place of God and man, faith and works, gospel and law. However, the scriptures seem to emphasize both elements—the primacy of God's loving gift and the need for man's response to the gift. Perhaps the solution ultimately lies in seeing the whole of salvation as completely dependent upon God's acting in his way and also dependent on man's acting in his way. What does a contemporary Christian understanding of the scriptures tell about man's response to the gift of God's love and man's part in the coming of the final stage of the reign of God?

The primary disposition on the part of man is openness to receive the gift of God's love. The fundamental human disposition is in accord with the primacy of God's love. The poor of Yahweh is always ready with outstretched arms to receive the mercy and love of God. In the New Testament the writers recall that Jesus became angry with only two groups of people. The attitude of Jesus to sinners and publicans shows no trace of wrath or anger. Jesus' anger is reserved for those who are not open to receive the gift of salvation—the Pharisees and the rich. Jesus cursed those who were hypocrites and smugly self-sufficient. The rich man who was content with what he owned and thought only about how he could store all his goods for the future was also condemned. He too was not open to receive the good news of God's love. Both the Pharisee and the rich man are content with their present lot; they believe they are doing all that is necessary. The sinner or publican who strikes his breast and asks for forgiveness is closer to the reign of God.

The Christian is ever open to the call of God in whatever form the call might come to him. Thus the necessity for the contemporary Christian to read the signs of the times. Openness characterizes the entire life of the follower of Jesus. The responsibility of the Christian is to hear the saving call of God and to respond to it. The scriptures constantly call for vigilance. The Christian is ever alert for the coming of the Lord whether it be in the form of the neighbor in poverty or hunger or in any kind of human need. The frequent call to vigilance in the New Testament is in accord with the basic disposition of openness to receive the saving mercy of God.

However, man's response to the gift of the reign of God involves more than just an openness to receive the gift. Man's response is to be total and complete. The follower of Jesus is called to leave all things to follow the Master. The true disciple cannot even try to serve two masters. A total giving to God and the neighbor in need points out the fullness of the response of the Christian to the call of God in Jesus. The very totality of the claim in general and the particular aspects of that claim in concrete circumstances indicate the radicalness of man's response. Conversion truly demands a change of heart in the Christian. Now the primary concern of the Christian becomes the neighbor in need. The Christian who has experienced the mercy and forgiveness of God must exhibit the same mercy and forgiveness to others. To be forgiven by God is not just a juridical fact. To be forgiven means that man has completely changed his own heart. The scriptures frequently stress the fact that true forgiveness from God means that the individual is now willing to forgive others the same way that Jesus has shown God's mercy to us.

In the "Our Father" we were taught to pray to God to forgive us our sins as we forgive those who trespass against us. The parable of the unmerciful servant recalls what is expected from one who has received the forgiveness of the Father. The servant had been forgiven a huge debt by his master; but the same servant was unwilling to forgive the comparatively insignificant debt of a fellow servant. The parable ends by reminding the readers that the heavenly Father will deal in the same way with us unless we are willing to forgive our brothers from our hearts (Matt 18:23-35). Through conversion to the reign of God the Christian has become a new creature in the life-giving Spirit and must now walk according to the new life that he has received in Christ Jesus. Anyone who meditates on the scriptures has to eliminate any type of quietism or denial of the importance of man's faith-issuing works. The problem created by the seemingly impossible and radical ethical demands of Jesus was discussed in Chapter One.

CONTINUAL CONVERSION

Conversion is not a once-for-all action. Continual growth and conversion mark the entire life of the Christian. The dynamism of the Christian life results from a number of factors. The openness which is the fundamental attitude of the Christian serves as the basis for continual growth and development. A continual openness means that the Christian can never be content with what he now does. The Christian is always looking for further development. No matter how long or well he lives, the Christian must always remain open for the call of God and neighbor. No static norms can ever express the fundamental vitality and dynamism of the Christian life.

The eschatological nature of the reign of God also calls

for a continual growth on the part of those who are sharing in the work of bringing about the final stage of the reign. The majority of Christian theologians today accept some type of inaugurated eschatology. The messianic or eschatological era has begun with the coming of Jesus. Men are now living in the "times in between the two comings of Jesus." The reign of Jesus is now present and pushing toward its final completion and perfection. The individual Christian is now called to participate in the work of bringing about the final stage of the reign of God. The follower of Jesus is caught up in the urgency of the reign of God which is inexorably pushing forward towards its final stage.

Conversion calls for a continual growth because man in this world is never totally converted. The Christian always remains, in the expression of Martin Luther, *simul justus et peccator*—at the same time just and sinful. Christian experience constantly reminds us that we are spiritual schizophrenics. Scriptural exegetes now question the application of Paul's dictum in Romans 7:21-23 to the already baptized Christian. Paul there speaks about the man who experiences the inner struggle within himself of doing the evil he does not want to do and not doing the good which he does want to do. Some scholars argue today that the Pauline saying refers to the man who is not yet baptized. However, the situation described by Paul is applicable to all of us as Christians. We all feel within ourselves our own selfishness and sinfulness continually warring against the impulse of *agape*. The scriptures themselves remind us of the tension in which we live. On the one hand, the scriptures speak glowingly of the new life we have received in Christ Jesus. The Christian now shares and participates in the joy and triumph of the Paschal mystery. St. John even claims that the Christian who remains in Christ Jesus cannot commit sin (1 John 5:18). On the other hand, the scriptures inculcate the need for struggle and growth. The weeds will continue to grow in the field. The tares and the wheat will grow together until the end of time. The whole world is still groaning, looking and waiting for the fullness of redemption. The Christian can never think that he has it made.

Theologically, one can explain the data of scripture and the Christian experience in terms of the Christian who still experiences sin within him. There is a struggle between light and darkness existing within our own hearts. Each and everyone of us experiences the sinfulness which is still part of our existence. Conversion is never fully accomplished. The Christian continually struggles to overcome the hardness and selfishness of his own heart. Our own sinfulness is a constant reminder that salvation is God's gift to us. At the same time our own sinfulness and hardness of heart form an impelling motive for growing in the love of God and neighbor. Our participation in the victory of Jesus over sin requires that we continually struggle to overcome the remains of sin in our own lives. The Christian who claims he is not a sinner is a liar (1 John 1:8). There are still the remains of sin in all of us, and we are called to share in the redeeming work of overcoming sin through love.

The documents of Vatican II have spoken eloquently about the pilgrim Church. Like the Church, the individual Christian is also a pilgrim. The pilgrim Church is in constant need of reformation, like the individual who is in need of continual conversion. Sin still exists to some extent in the pilgrim Church and in the pilgrim Christian. Roman Catholic theology speaks of the four marks of the Church: one, holy, Catholic, and apostolic. Perhaps we could add a fifth mark to the Church. The Church is one, holy, Catholic, apostolic, and sinful. Yes, the Church is the bride of Christ and the People of God; but the Church embraces us sinful people. The Church is never perfectly faithful to its spouse. The sinful Church is in constant need of reformation and change. However, the individual Christian can never look with disdain on the sinful Church because he himself also experiences his own sinfulness. The pilgrim Christian continually strives to grow closer to his goal of perfect union with God and neighbor. The sinfulness of the Christian is a constant reminder of the gift of salvation from God and the need for an ever greater cooperation and growth in the love of God.

Roman Catholic theology has traditionally maintained that the person in the state of grace still commits venial sin. However, theology often forgot the implication of that realization for the continual growth of the Christian. European writers have called attention to an inadequate explanation of the sinfulness which every baptized Christian continues to experience. Some writers refer to "the mystique of sin" which appears perhaps more in literature than as a theory presented in theological works. The mystique of sin is a reaction against the pharisaical attitude that occasionally characterizes the so-called good Christian. The true Christian realizes that he is a sinner. According to the mystique of sin, man is closest to God when he is broken and crying out from the depths for mercy. Any attempt to do good merely makes man hypocritical and actually puts an obstacle between himself and God. Man is never closer to God than when he realizes his own sinfulness and cries out for forgiveness. The mystique of sin is correct in calling attention to man's constant need of forgiveness and mercy. However, such a theory forgets the healing and redeeming aspect of God's love. The Christian who has experienced the love of God is truly changed and must now act in accord with the new life he has received. However, the change of conversion is not yet perfect. Thus the Christian is called to grow continually in his love and gradually try to overcome the sinfulness and selfishness which remain in his heart. The notion of continual conversion and growth avoids the one extreme of pharisaical self-righteousness and the other extreme of the mystique of sin.

COSMIC DIMENSION OF THE REIGN OF GOD

Perhaps the most important characteristic of conversion and the reign of God today is the social and cosmic dimension. The Christian attitude in the past has been too often unilaterally individualistic and personal. Salvation is a matter that affects man's soul. Religion and Christianity pertain only to the private realm of man's life. There has been a separation between man's daily life in the world and his understanding of the meaning of Christianity. Today theology is more conscious of the need to relate Christianity to daily living. The Vatican Council has deplored the split between faith and daily life (The Pastoral Constitution on the Church in the Modern World, n. 42). Christian theologians today are speaking of secularity and the relationship of history and human progress to the reign of God.

There are a number of factors which have influenced the lack of a social and cosmic dimension to conversion in the past. One factor prominent in the Catholic tradition has been an attitude which does not attribute much importance to the material and this-worldly aspect of human life. An important influence that underrated the value of life in this world was the *fuga mundi* (flight from the world) spirituality which developed in early Christianity with the rise of monasticism. Such a spirituality in itself is not wrong, for it does point out one aspect of the reign of God. The problem arose from the fact that such a spirituality became identified with the only true way of striving for Christian perfection. The world was considered incompatible with the fullness of the Christian vocation. At best, the world was neutral and man's daily life did not contribute anything to the reign of God.

The rather negative attitude towards life in the world is well illustrated in the custom of basket weaving which arose among the early monks in Egypt. The early monks left the world and fled into the desert for a life of prayer and contemplation. However, the monks could not spend all day in prayer. To fill in the hours of the day they began to weave baskets. The monks did not take their newly woven baskets to the nearest market to sell them. Rather, after weaving a basket, the monk would then take the basket apart and then put it together again. The only real purpose in basket weaving was to fill in the idle hours of the day! Basket weaving was busy work which gave the monks something to do during the hours they were not praying. Unfortunately, most of man's activities in his daily life were put into the class of basket weaving. No matter what he did, man was not really contributing to the reign of God. Human existence here in the world was just a matter of waiting for the eschaton to come. One might compare existence in this world to the attitude of passengers waiting at an airport for a delayed flight to depart. People are just whiling away the hours waiting for the plane to take off. They may walk around the terminal aimlessly, or scan through the same paper for the tenth time, or just sit and stare with a very dull expression in their eyes. They are just trying to pass the hours waiting for the plane. Too often the Christian life in this world has been merely a question of filling in the years waiting for the plane to take off for eternity. A one-sided *fuga mundi* spirituality said nothing about the Christian meaning of man's daily life in the world. Only in the last few decades has Catholic theology tried to develop a spirituality of life in the world and a theology of the world, history, and human progress.

A Greek philosophical prejudice against materiality also affected the Christian's understanding of the material world and man's existence on this earth. According to the Platonic concepts, the body is the prison of the soul. Happiness obviously consists in freeing oneself from the body and returning to the world of ideas and contemplation. Material things are looked down upon as hindrances and obstacles to the higher part of man—his soul. The material universe was really an obstacle to the full development of man's higher life. Such a pejorative attitude towards materiality definitely colored the Christian outlook. Many remnants of the Greek mentality have continued to exist in Christian thought. Look at the concept of heaven and eternal beatitude which has been proposed. The Catholic vision of heaven seems to depend too much on a Greek concept of happiness. Christian theology has always taught the spiritual or mystical union which exists between God and the Christian. However, the way of achieving such union was proposed almost unilaterally in terms of contemplation. Theologians today are beginning to think that such a union can also be achieved through loving service of others. Contemplation is necessary and important but perhaps not the only way of achieving union with God. The Greek notion of history also was not favorable to a theology of history and man's participation in the ongoing work of history. Although the Hebraic mind had a linear view of history, the Greek concept of history was cyclic. History was not really heading towards any particular end point but only repeating itself in never-ending cycles. Thus man's salvation could be found only in being delivered from this present world and being assumed into the world above history.

A third factor influencing the negative attitude of Christian thinking towards the importance of human life in the present world was the overly spiritualistic heresies which have constantly plagued the Church throughout its history. The historical recurrence of such thinking shows the fascination which such an approach has for the human mind. A dualism which in some ways looks down upon the material part of man has frequently appeared in the history of the Church. From the earliest influences of Manicheanism down to the Jansenism of the last few centuries Christianity has not been able to retain a balanced understanding of man's corporality and materiality. An illustration of the negative attitude towards the material is shown in the meaning frequently mentioned by Christian preachers and teachers, even today, to the biblical concept of flesh. The Pauline notions of spirit and flesh do not correspond to spirit and matter as the component parts of man. Flesh is not a pejorative term referring to the material part of man. According to the Pauline usage, flesh and spirit both refer to the whole man (body and soul, if you will). The spirit is the whole man insofar as he is under the power and direction of the Spirit. The flesh is the whole man insofar as he is under the power of sin and selfishness. A dualism with pejorative connotations for the material part of man and the universe has unduly influenced the Christian attitude towards the life of man in the world.

Catholic theology also favored a negative attitude towards the world and existence in the world by developing a notion of two classes of Christians. Those Christians who were called to perfection embraced the vows and the religious life to unite themselves more closely to God. However, the vast majority of Christians were not called to such perfection and holiness but were only called to live in the world and obey the commandments. The Ten Commandments obliged all Christians, but those who embraced the religious life were vowed to perfection through the following of the evangelical counsels. Life in the world was not a way of seeking Christian perfection. All that was required of the ordinary Christian living in the world was the observation of the Commandments. However, the far greater part of the ordinary life of the Christian in the world was outside the pale of his Christian faith and had nothing to do with his faith.

The Constitution on the Church has corrected the poor emphases of the past by recalling the teaching of Jesus that *all* Christians are called to perfection. Since all Christians are called to perfection, one cannot flatly assert that this pertains only to people who take the religious vows. Christian perfection consists in charity—love of God and neighbor. The vows are only means to arrive at that goal. The vows do not refer primarily to the goal which is the same for all Christians, but rather the vows describe the means by which certain people try to achieve their goal. The danger always exists of making means into ends. Perhaps the greatest form of idolatry is to absolutize what is only the way or the means to the end. Even in the living of religious life under the vows, the vows were frequently treated as ends in themselves. The vows are meaningful only to the extent that they lead the religious to a greater union with God and neighbor. They have no real meaning in themselves for their own sake but only insofar as they lead to a greater and more effective charity. Other people may choose other means to arrive at the goal of the Christian life which is the same for all followers of Jesus. St. Thomas himself taught that the vows are means of overcoming some of the obstacles which lie on the road to Christian perfection, which is charity or union with God and neighbor.

Another fallacy has seen the vows as adding something to the ordinary Christian life. I would prefer to see the vows in terms of a specification rather than a quantitative addition. The primary vow for all Christians is the baptismal vow. Baptism marks the conversion of the Christian. The change of heart in baptism is well represented by the baptismal vow which is now generally made in a very perfunctory manner by the godparents. The Christian at baptism vows to give himself totally to the new life he has received in Christ Jesus and to renounce the attractions of sin and selfishness. Any subsequent vows in the Christian life merely specify the primary vow of baptism. There are different ways in which different individuals can live out their baptismal vows. The majority of Christians specify their baptismal vow through their marriage vow; others through the vows of the religious life. However, the additional vows add nothing quantitatively to the promise of baptism.

One argument previously given for the superiority of the life of the vows centers on the direct approach to God which is found in a life under the religious vows. Religious life under the vows consecrates one to God directly. The person without vows has other cares and persons which must preoccupy him or her. The married person must also be worried about his spouse and children, whereas the religious is directly united with God through the vows. The person in the world loves God indirectly through other persons, whereas the religious is directly consecrated to God. However, there seems to be a fallacy in such an argument. Can anyone assert that Jesus loved his heavenly Father less because he also loved all men at the same time? Jesus' love for man in no way detracted from his love for the Father. The argument about the direct or indirect way to God seems to confuse what scholastic theology called the material and the formal object of love. The material object comprises the persons who are loved by us. The formal object is the motivating force of our love. If Christian *agape* is the formal object of our love, then the different people who are embraced by such *agape* do not detract from our love for the Father. In fact, the unique characteristic of *agape* is the fact of its universal character so that *agape* should embrace as many as possible. Loving others with *agape* in no way detracts from our love for God.

The reasons mentioned thus far for the lack of a cosmic and this-worldly dimension to the Christian life pertain primarily to Roman Catholic thinking. However, Protestant theology has also failed to develop a spirituality of the Christian living in the world. There were other influences operative in the Protestant tradition which contributed to the separation of the Christian's faith and his daily life. The theological notion of the corruption of sin detracted from the meaning and value of the world and earthly realities. Catholic theology in the past has frequently caricatured the idea of the total depravity or total corruption found in Protestant thinking. However, the emphasis on sin as corrupting everything in the world naturally is in accord with a pessimistic attitude toward the world. The two-realm or two-kingdom theory of Luther also tended to separate man's private religious life from his public life or life in the world. According to the theory of the two kingdoms, the political and social world is separated from the private world of faith. The private world of faith and the personal life of man is under the gospel—the good news of the saving activity of God in Christ. The political and social life of man is under the law. The law exists primarily to provide a dike against the presence of sin. The law is not able to overcome sin, but the law tries to contain sin as best it can. The gospel has little or no relationship with the political and social life of man. The magistrates and the state are to be obeyed in all that pertains to the social and political orders. Even the injustices of the social order are to be suffered in patience, for God even uses sinners for his own good purposes. The two-kingdoms theory parallels the dichotomy between gospel and law and between redemption and creation. One can dispute what was the real teaching of Luther on this point, but pietistic Protestant tendencies have tried to interpret Luther as a basis for their contention that the gospel is directed to the individual, and the sole task of the Church is to proclaim man's reconciliaion with a merciful God through Christ Jesus. The pietistic attitude still exists in some Protestant circles today.

The evangelism crusades definitely share the mentality that the primary and only function of the Church is proclaiming individual salvation through the merciful love of God.

Christian theology, both Roman Catholic and Protestant, until comparatively recently has not developed a spirituality of the Christian living in the world. In the nineteenth century theology did begin to realize the social and cosmic dimension of the reign of God. The above-mentioned reasons at least partially explain the absence of a theology and spirituality of life in the world. There were strands in both Catholic and Protestant thinking which are more open to an understanding of the role and life of the Christian in the world. Lutheran theology has constantly emphasized the vocation of the individual. Catholic theology has upheld the goodness of the natural which should include an appreciation of worldly values. Perhaps in previous centuries the social and cultural conditions were such that the Christian theologies could not fully appreciate the social and cosmic dimensions of conversion and the reign of God. Perhaps it is only in our own times that the cosmic dimension of the reign of God has been forcing itself upon the consciousness of Christian thinkers.

Too often we Christians fail to realize the changes which have taken place in the modern world. Today, when the vast majority of people are being educated, there is a reservoir of knowledge both quantitatively and qualitatively that can be tapped to deal with the problems which affect the world as a whole. The democratic revolution which first swept France and America in the eighteenth century has just recently come to the continent of Africa. The industrial revolution has completely changed the culture of society. Communication and transportation have now shrunk the size of the earth. Continents are now more closely linked today than cities were two centuries ago. The scientific and technical revolutions have given man a power he never before even thought he could possess. Thus modern culture and civilization have made the contemporary Christian more aware of the cosmic dimension of the reign of God.

Take, as an example, the question of poverty. Conditions of the twentieth century have made us aware of the problems of poverty. People in the United States see on their television sets racial violence that in many ways is attributed to the poverty existing in our cities. Any man who reads the daily newspaper is aware of the fact that two-thirds of the world lives in hunger. Today we are much more conscious of the problems created by poverty. Even more important, today we are able to do something about the problem of poverty. Human resources and technology are now able to overcome the problem of poverty in the world. In these circumstances the Christian meditating on the gospels can see that he has a new task before him. The problem of world poverty is a moral issue. The Christian has a responsibility to overcome such poverty.

The flexibility that the gospel authors show in their use of the beatitudes should serve as an excellent illustration for the Christian living today. Jesus proclaimed happiness for the poor and the hungry. Both Luke and Matthew adapted that proclamation of happiness to the needs of the people they were addressing. How could Luke possibly say that the poor and hungry were happy? Luke's solution was to admit that now such people are not happy, but in the future the poor and the hungry will find their happiness. However, the good news must be preached to the poor and the hungry in a different way today. Christian love for the neighbor in need has always called for a sharing of what we have with the poor. However, today the Christian is able to share much more than a tunic or a piece of clothing. Today, the Christian and all men of good will are able to overcome the problem of world poverty. The way to solve the problem is not simple. Christian responsibility calls for an understanding of all the complicated problems involved and a competency derived from a knowledge of the appropriate social and empirical sciences. However, Christian love for the poor can supply the necessary motivation to move the hearts and minds of men to work toward a solution to the problem of world poverty.

Conditions of modern life have made it possible for man to see more clearly the social and cosmic dimensions of the reign of God in the last century or so. Christians meditatively reflecting on reality have asked questions about the meaning of their efforts in daily life. Do art, culture, science, technology, and human accomplishment have any relationship to the reign of God? Or are they just examples of busy work? Do man's efforts in his daily life bear any positive relationship to the realization of the reign of God in Christ? Contemporary Christians have reacted against a spirituality or conversion that was one-sidedly eschatological. According to the eschatological approach, the reign of God was God's saving gift that would appear at the end of time and with no real relationship or continuity to what man was doing in his daily life. However, Christians today speak of an incarnational spirituality which sees the reign of God as the gift of God and as the work of man here and now cooperating in bringing about the new heaven and the new earth.

Note the inadequacies in contrasting an eschatological approach and an incarnational approach to the Christian life. A proper understanding of eschatological is not opposed to the notion of incarnational. Eschatology does not merely refer to what will happen at the end of time .The contemporary understanding of eschatological embraces the present world insofar as the eschatological reign of God is already present and going forward to the final consummation of the world and history at the second coming of Christ. The question in terms of eschatological versus incarnational is a pseudo-problem. The attitude of the Christian toward the meaning of life in this world as described below tries to correspond to the proper understanding of eschatology which sees the eschatological reign of God already present and pushing forward to the final stage of the reign of God which will be both inside and outside history. I have occasionally retained the older and very inadequate terminology only because such terminology has been used by Catholic theologians in the last few decades.

THE CHRISTIAN ATTITUDE TOWARD THIS WORLD

Man's relationship to the world is not merely that of renunciation or flight from the world. The Christian is called to transform the world and to cooperate in bringing about the final stage of the reign of God. The relationship between this world and the final stage of the reign of God is not merely a relationship of discontinuity. There is some continuity between this world and the next. What man does for the betterment of the world and human society is a promotion of the reign of God in Christ. The attitude of the Christian toward the present is not totally negative or pessimistic. There is a positive orientation of human reality here and now towards the final stage of the reign of God in Christ.

There are many theological arguments supporting the more positive view of man's life in this world as contributing towards the final stage of the reign of God. Man in his daily efforts cooperates with God in bringing about the new heaven and the new earth. Life in the world is not just a matter of busy work to while away the hours but rather a positive cooperation in working for the reign of God. The mystery of the Incarnation furnishes the cornerstone for the basis of an incarnational spirituality. Material things do belong to the mystery of God's loving reign. The world is intimately joined to the mystery of salvation. Jesus himself took the world and the human enterprise seriously by becoming man.

The entire mystery of salvation shows the cosmic and social aspect of the reign of God. Sin itself has an effect on the world. Sin, according to the Genesis account, not only affected man in his relationship with God; but sin also affected man in his relationship with his fellow man and with the whole world. Adam and Eve, according to the mythical narration of Genesis, were made to share their lives in the unity of love in one flesh. The author points out the effect of sin on their relationship. Did Adam try to protect and defend his wife? No. Adam's first reaction was to point an accusing finger at Eve and blame her for the fault so that he could escape blame and guilt. Sin had affected their relationship. The destructive power of sin is seen in its effect on the relationship of the children of Adam and Eve. Cain killed Abel. The first eleven chapters of Genesis are really a history of sin, as man constantly falls under its sway despite occasional interventions by God.

Sin also affected Adam and Eve in their relationship with the cosmos. Before sin there is great harmony existing between Adam and lower creation. This harmony is signified by the fact that Adam gave a name to all the beasts of the field signifying their dependence on him. However, after sin Adam experiences the toil and suffering connected with work. No longer is the world malleable in his hands, but rather earth seems to resist his efforts and make him struggle and suffer in his attempt to subdue the rebellious cosmos. Sin also affects Eve in that which is most characteristically female. Henceforth, she will bring forth her children in pain and sorrow. Nature itself would resist the childbearing process and cause suffering. The social and cosmic aspects of sin in Genesis are dynamic. Sin grows as a force in the world so that other people are easily brought under its sway. Sin pollutes the air men breathe and becomes incarnate in the very structures of human life and society so that men are unable to avoid sin. We know from our own experience how difficult it is for an honest Christian witness in some aspects of life because of the corruption and dishonesty which seem to be taken for granted. So strong is the cosmic and social aspect of sin that theologians are now considering original sin and its passage from one generation to another in terms of the sin of the world.

Since sin has a cosmic effect, redemption too embraces the whole world. The first chapter of Colossians speaks about Christ as the image of all creation and the head of the Church. In him all things are tied together. "Through him God chose to reconcile the whole universe to himself, making peace through the shedding of his blood upon the cross— to reconcile all things, whether on earth or in heaven, through him alone" (Col 1:20). The letter to the Ephesians also stresses that through Christ the whole universe, all in heaven and on earth, is brought into a unity (Eph 1:9-10). The letter to the Romans affirms that all creation is awaiting the fullness of its redemption. The universe was subject to frustration in sin, but the universe too is to share in redemption and enter into the joyous liberty of the children of God (Rom 8:18-25). Redemption thus has a cosmic dimension which cannot be forgotten in the Christian life. The Christian is called not only to change his own heart but also to change the social, political, economic, and cultural structures of human existence. Conversion is not addressed to the heart alone.

The story of salvation reaches its climax in the parousia. But there is a relationship of continuity between this world and the next. Even the apocalyptic literature speaks about a new heaven and a new earth, but the newness retains a continuity (although not necessarily a perfect continuity) with what has gone before. The new heaven and the new earth will not completely descend ready-made from above, but rather man is called now to cooperate in shaping the final stage of the reign of God. Theologians note three different types of eschatological theory which seem to appear in the scriptures and in theology: the apocalyptic, the teleological, and the prophetic. Christian eschatology must embrace all three aspects. A purely apocalyptic eschatology would eliminate the cooperation of man bringing about the new heaven and the new earth, but the other eschatological theories all entail some continuity between the present existence of mankind and the future.

The sacramental celebration of redemption also indicates the cosmic dimension of the reign of God. The sacramental principle follows from the incarnation. God's favor and love come to man in a visible and historical form. The incarnation brought material things into the plan of redemption. The sacramental celebration of salvation points to the same cosmic dimension. Basic human elements such as bread, wine, water, and oil are brought into the celebration. The sacraments themselves are signs not only of the historical redemptive work of Jesus but also of the future perfection of the work of salvation. The sacraments point to the future. There is a connection and continuity between the historical event of the past, the present celebration of redemption, and the final stage of the reign of God. The incarnation and the sacramental principle dovetail very well with the psychosomatic nature of man. Man is not just a pure spirit. Man is intimately connected with his environment and the cosmos.

Theologies of creation and history also point to the place of the cosmos in the future stage of the reign of God. Creation is now seen in the framework of evolutionary theory. Creation is not a once-for-all process such as was described in Genesis. Rather, creation is a continual process. The fullness of creation is not in Genesis but rather in the Apocalypse, the last book of the scriptures, which describes the end and the fullness of creation. The last few decades have seen a marked increase in the interest in the theology of history. History is not just a meaningless, never-ending cycle; but rather history is continually developing towards its fulfillment. The progress and achievement in human life have made man more aware of the progressive understanding of history and creation.

The insistence on the immanence of God and the theology of secularity also are indications of the cosmic dimensions of salvation. A change in the emphasis in ecclesiology likewise manifests a greater appreciation of worldly and secular values. An older theology tended to identify the Church and the Kingdom of God. In such a world view, the world itself had little or no value. Now theology speaks of the Church as the servant of the world. The world does not exist to serve the Church and keep the Church going; rather, the Church exists to serve the world and promote the true values of the world. In a certain sense, the Church belongs to the times in between and will cease to exist when the fullness of time arrives. However, then the world will not only continue to exist; the world will exist in all its fullness and splendor in the new creation.

Thus the cosmic dimension of the reign of God and conversion illustrates the importance of man's cooperation in building the new heaven and the new earth. Man's human activities are not mere basket weaving or whiling away the hours with busy work waiting for the kingdom to descend from above. However, there is also the danger of falling into a naive optimism and progressivism. Christian theology has definite safeguards against such a naive and simplistic approach to human existence. In general, the theological limitations to a complete continuity between this world and the next stem from the limitations and sinfulness of man and also from an eschatology which definitely holds for some discontinuity between man's efforts and the final state of the reign of God.

The sense of progress and growth towards the new heaven and the new earth is not always readily perceptible. There will be frustrations and obstacles precisely because of limitations and sin. In any Christian life there is always room for the cross and the Paschal Mystery. Suffering and frustration will confront the Christian as he tries to make human life more human. The transformation of the world involves man's participation in the Paschal Mystery of dying and rising. Hope in the saving word and work of God gives the Christian the strength to continue despite opposition, frustrations, and frequent setbacks. The cross of Christ casts its shadow and its light over every human endeavor.

Not everything that arises in the world is good. There is a danger for the Christian in becoming too conformed to the social, cultural, political, and economic structures of a given nation or a given period of history. The greatest idolatry is to absolutize what is merely a very historically limited reality. The prophetic aspect of Christian eschatology calls for the Christian to continually criticize and perfect the structures of human existence. "Perfect" might even be too weak a word. At times, the revolution of structures is asked of the Christian. An article has recently appeared entitled: "Metanoia: The Moral Principle of the Christian Revolution."[3] The world can set up its own idols. The Christian going towards the new heaven and the new earth always has to judge the earthly structures critically and try to transform them into more human dimensions. The prophetic Christian life in the world cannot merely accept uncritically the moods or structures which appear in human culture and life.

Man's cooperation in the coming of the new heaven and the new earth is essential and necessary but not sufficient. There will still be some discontinuity between man's efforts and the final state of the kingdom. There are always two aspects to the reign of God—his gift and man's cooperation. There is at times a danger of forgetting that the reign is his gift. The true Christian in the world can never develop the Messiah complex that so often characterizes persons and movements in history. One wonders, for example, if American foreign policy has not suffered from a Messiah complex. The attitude seems to be that America is the agent of God to bring peace and stability to the whole world. The United States does have a grave responsibility in the world, but perhaps our country has at times overplayed its role.

Man living in the 1960's is most open to the progressive development of the reign of God. However, at other periods of time men were not so optimistic. The mood of the world immediately after World War II was entirely different. One wonders if such a world could have ever accepted the optimistic progressivism of a Teilhard, for example. After that war, men were very conscious of the existence and the power of sin in the world. Man's inhumanity to man had been experienced in two world wars within thirty years of history. Even today, man can too easily forget the existence of sin and evil in our world. Certain parts of America may be enjoying great prosperity, but the urban riots point up a huge social evil existing in our country. The poverty and misery of most of the world cries out to God for vengeance in the light of the prosperity and wealth that others enjoy. One can all to easily forget the power of sin.

Likewise, progress in science and technology can too easily lull men into thinking that all progress is always continuous.

Scientific advancements do build on past triumphs for an even greater future development. However, this is not true in the more human areas of man's existence. Progress in art and culture is not necessarily in a straight line of development. Perhaps the music and art of a much earlier century is better than the art and music of today. The matter is at least open to debate. Progressivism in technology and the sciences should not lull the Christian into expecting the same type of unilateral development in the more human work of building the new heaven and the new earth.

Not all men share the sense of creativity in contributing to the development of the reign of God. In fact, the vast majority of mankind today do not share that creative joy. There is a danger of the elite talking among themselves from their own limited experience in discussing the cooperation of man in building the new heaven and the new earth. However, the future does hold a greater promise for furnishing many more people with the necessary requisites for contributing in a creative way to the new heaven and the new earth. Optimism and progress characterize the Christian's attitude towards the cosmic dimension of redemption, but the Christian vision constantly tempers that optimism with the reality of human limitations and sinfulness.

Conversion has many aspects and dimensions. As the central moral message of the New Testament, the Christian message of conversion must be properly understood in all its manifold dimensions. This section has emphasized especially the dynamic aspect of continual conversion and the social and cosmic dimensions of such conversion. The entire chapter has not really tried to solve theoretically the problem of bringing together the role of God and the role of man in the work of conversion. It has maintain the need for both. However, existentially in his own life each Christian must bring the two together. The radical ethical demands of Jesus actually help the Christian to bring together the aspect of the reign of God as God's gift and its aspect of man's cooperation. The Christian always tries to achieve the goal outlined in the ethics of Jesus. Although constantly falling short, the Christian thus realizes his own need for continual forgiveness and receives the hope that is necessary in continuing his own efforts despite the frustrations and oppositions he experiences in himself and in the world of people and things around him. Thus the radical ethics of Jesus are both gospel and law, gift and demand. In continually striving to come closer to the ideal proposed by Jesus, the Christian experiences both the reality of God's merciful love and man's own cooperation in bringing about the new heaven and the new earth. The gospel call to conversion is in all its dimensions the central moral teaching of Jesus.

Notes for Chapter 2

1.
Jacques Dupont O.S.B., *Les Beatitudes* (Editions de l'Abbaye de Saint-André, Bruges, 1954). In 1958 he published an extensive revision of the literary question of the beatitudes. I have followed Dupont's ideas quite closely.
2.
A somewhat similar modern parable is found in Paul Ramsey, *Basic Christian Ethics* (Charles Scribner's Sons, 1950), 70.
3.
Oswald Dijkstra, "Metanoia: The Moral Principle of the Christian Revolution," *The Clergy Monthly*, 30 (1966), 457-467. Also see Richard Shaull, "Revolutionary Change in Theological Perspective," in *Christian Social Ethics in a Changing World*, ed. John C. Bennett (Association Press, 1966), 23-43; also Emilio Castro, "Conversion and Social Transformation," *op. cit.*, 348-366.

Absolute Norms in
Moral Theology

Chapter Three

Catholic moral theology generally defends the existence of absolute and universally valid norms for Christian ethical behavior. In the last few years a renewal of moral theology has taken place, but the renewal has merely accepted the existence of certain absolute norms. The *aggiornamento* in moral theology stresses that, within the boundary lines marked off by absolute norms binding on all, there exists a large area of moral conduct which is not governed by the application of general norms to particular cases. Bernard Häring has emphasized the concept of *kairos*.[1] Karl Rahner has spoken about a formal existentialist ethic.[2] Contemporary moral theology realizes that all men are called to perfection in the reign of God and that theology can no longer be content to discover the dividing line between sin and no sin. The biblical, liturgical, and catechetical renewals in the Catholic Church have influenced the outlook and scope of moral theology. Personalism and an emphasis on conscience characterize the recent developments in moral theology. Contemporary Catholic moral theology can no longer be accused of legalism and negativism on a wide scale.

However, there still remains the question about universal, absolute, negative norms of Christian conduct (e.g., divorce, direct abortion, euthanasia, sterilization, artificial insemination, etc.). I personally have the feeling that even in this area there has been an inflation of absolutes. Is Roman Catholic theology irrevocably committed to the existence of such absolute norms in moral theology? What is the reason that explains the existence of absolutes in Catholic theology? The purpose of the present essay is to show that Roman Catholic theology is not unalterably committed to a generic insistence on absolute norms in ethical conduct. The first section of the essay will examine the two alleged sources of absolutism in Roman Catholic theology—the natural law and the teaching authority of the Church.[3] The second section of the paper will propose two other factors that have contributed to the existence of absolutes in Catholic moral thought.

I. THE NATURAL LAW IN CATHOLIC THEOLOGY

Both Protestant and Catholic theologians agree that the Roman Catholic teaching on natural law is one of the prime factors for the existence of universal, absolute norms.[4] I shall try to show that the theory of the natural law and the teaching of such a theory in the Catholic Church does not necessarily mean that Catholic theology must always admit universal norms of behavior which are true in all cases. First I will attempt to show that the term natural law does not designate a coherent philosophical system with an agreed upon body of content which has been in existence in the Catholic Church from the beginning. Secondly, I do not think that in what is by far the larger part of its moral teaching the Catholic Church has used natural law as a vehicle in determining the morality of a particular action.

AN HISTORICAL INVESTIGATION

An historical investigation is necessary to show that natural law does not designate a monolithic philosophical system with an agreed upon code of ethical conduct which has existed throughout the history of the Catholic Church. Although Aristotle made many contributions to the Thomistic concept of natural law, Aristotle never explicitly formulated a natural law doctrine.[5] Aristotle maintains that every living organism has its own nature which is teleological, dynamic and specific. The growth toward which it tends is the perfection of the organism itself, but this perfection is specific and not individual. For example, each dog tends to develop into the ideal exemplar of the species of dog except insofar as it is impeded by extrinsic circumstances (disease, other killing animals, etc.). However, with regard to man Aristotle did not accept any intrinsic dynamism which propels man toward his goal of rational perfection. Although Aristotle describes man as having a desire for happiness and self-realization, man has no intrinsic principle of operation which necessarily leads him to his goal. Man's success in obtaining his goal depends more on favorable extrinsic circumstances (such as health, wealth, friends, etc.) and does not depend on an intrinsic, dynamic tendency to perfection.

Commentators often point to the stoical period as one of the high points in natural law development.[6] However, even among the stoics natural law is not monolithic. In general, the Stoics, like Aristotle, shared a rational view of reality. But whereas Aristotle stressed the individual substance as the principle of intelligibility, the Stoics looked upon the universe as the unit of intelligibility. Happiness or virtue then consisted in having a right relationship with the universe, the cosmos.[7] The stoic philosophers did employ the term natural law, but natural law did not designate a coherent philosophical system. According to one Catholic scholar, natural law for the Stoics was a generic term much like the term morality in our day. Stoic philosophers believed that right and wrong can be applied to human actions just as true and false can be applied to the area of human knowledge; but they disagreed among themselves on the ethical goodness or evil of particular actions.[8] Some Stoics are reputed to have held that the wise man at times can find sufficient reasons to justify the taking of his life. Zeno definitely maintained that among the wise there should be a community of wives with a free choice of partners. Chrysippus is quoted by Sextus Empiricus as approving those practices in which the mother has children by her son and the father has children by his daughter. Some of the stoic philosophers were accused of permitting masturbation, homosexuality, and prostitution. Perhaps these accusations against the stoic philosophers are polemical and exaggerated, but they at least indicate that the natural law for the Stoics did not include an agreed upon code of ethical conduct. Although a general agreement in thinking about morality existed among the Stoics, the agreement did not always extend to the morality of particular actions.[9]

Roman law adopted and used the notion of natural law, but in Roman law there were also different ways of understanding natural law. Gaius (about 160) distinguished two types of law: the *ius civile* which is proper to each country; and the *ius gentium*, the common heritage of all humanity which is known through natural reason.[10] Gaius meant by *ius gentium* what philosophers today mean by natural law. Ulpian (+228) proposed a threefold division of law. The *ius civile* is again the proper law of the given community, but Ulpian divides the more universal law into two parts. The *ius naturale* is the rule of actions common to man and all the animals, such as the union of the sexes and the procreation and education of offspring. Ulpian uses the term *ius naturae* to designate the work of nature apart from every rational intervention. The *ius gentium*, as the common heritage of all the people, is the work of human reason. For example, before any human intervention men were born free; but then wars occurred, and by *iure gentium* slavery arose.[11] Among the Roman jurists the *ius gentium* was to some extent a human institution, but not in the same sense as the *ius civile*. Man's reason establishes the *ius gentium* by conforming to the natural order of things through the human instinct which is common to all when it comes to the necessities of human existence.

In the development of the concept of natural law, the Scholastic period, and in particular Thomas Aquinas, have greatly influenced Catholic moral teaching. Thomas did not invent the natural law, but he found the concept existing among the theologians, philosophers, and jurists who lived before him. In fact, in his writings, Thomas cites four definitions of the natural law from older authorities, and all these definitions are different! Certainly before Thomas Aquinas there was no monolithic philosophical system called the natural law. Thomas cites the definition proposed by Cicero (*ius naturae est quod non opinio genuit sed quaedam innata vis inseruit*).[12] Thomas also refers to Ulpian's definition of the natural law as that which is common to man and all the animals apart from any intervention of reason.[13] Perhaps many of the problems in contemporary Catholic explanations of the natural law stem from Ulpian's definition which tends to identify the natural law with brute natural facticity. Man must respect the laws of nature and cannot interfere with them. But does not man's rationality demand that at times he interfere with the laws of nature so that he might live a more human existence? Particularly in the area of marital ethics Ulpian's concept of the natural law has created problems. Nature teaches both man and the animals that sexual union exists for the procreation and education of offspring. Animals know nothing about the love union aspect of sexuality. Consequently, Catholic thought stresses procreation as the primary end of marriage with the love union aspect of sexuality as the secondary end added on to what was primary and fundamental. Ulpian's definition seems to favor a dichotomy between nature and reason and gives primary importance to what is natural before any interference from reason.

Thomas also cites the definition of natural law proposed by Isidore of Seville—*ius naturale est commune omnium nationum*.[14] Although Isidore accepted the threefold division of law proposed by Ulpian, he modified the concept of *ius naturale*. The *ius naturale* is that which is common to all nations because it results not from any positive human institution but from the inclination and instinct of human nature itself. Isidore thus seems to avoid the dichotomy of separating in man the rational element from that which is common to man and all the animals. The notion of *ius gentium* for Isidore corresponds to the modern concept of international law and includes such things as wars and treaties.[15]

Thomas also quotes the definition of natural law proposed by Gratian, the monk who codified the laws of the Church in the twelfth century.[16] Gratian approvingly cites a text from Isidore to show that the human race is ruled by two things, natural law and customs (*moribus*). The natural law comprises two fundamental norms: do unto others what you would want them to do unto you; and do not do to others what you would not want them to do to you. However, Gratian then introduces some confusion into the matter by adopting a historical view which says that the natural law as found in these two norms is what is contained in the law and the gospel.[17]

The Decretists who commented upon the *Decree* of Gratian are not in accord about accepting Ulpian's definition. Among theologians, Albert the Great categorically rejects the definition of Ulpian, while St. Bonaventure espouses it. St. Thomas on this point follows the Franciscan master rather than his own teacher. The decretists and theologians of the twelfth and thirteenth centuries were also influenced by the school of Anselm of Laon. According to Anselm, the natural law as the primitive law of humanity, which existed even before the detailed prescriptions of the decalogue, can be reduced to the obligation to do good to others and to avoid evil. The natural law reduced to such immediately evident principles is an innate law written on the hearts of man by God the author of all nature.[18]

THOMAS AQUINAS

In his *Commentary on the Sentences* (1254-1256) Thomas cites the definitions proposed by Cicero, Ulpian, and Gratian. Thomas here accepts the definition proposed by Ulpian, but tries to modify its brute facticity by interpreting it as what natural reason says about those things which are common to man and all animals (*In IV Sent.*, d.33, q.1, a.1, ad 4um). In his *Commentary on the Ethics of Aristotle*, Thomas accepts the Greek philosopher's twofold division of *iustum naturale* and *iustum legale*, but he reconciles such a division with the threefold division of Ulpian. Ulpian's *ius civile* is Aristotle's *iustum legale*. Ulpian divides Aristotle's *iustum naturale* into that which is common to man and all the animals (*ius naturale* in the strictest sense) and that which is rational in man *(ius gentium)*. Thomas thus attempts to reconcile the Aristotelian and Ulpian concepts.[19]

Thomas begins his treatise on the division of human law in the *Summa Theologiae* by citing Isidore who divided all laws into divine and human laws. Isidore put natural law under the divine law, but human law embraced both the *ius civile* and the *ius gentium*. But how can the *ius gentium* be placed under human law while the natural law is placed under divine law? Did not Thomas himself in his *Commentary* say that the *ius gentium* is the rational part of the natural law? As usual, Thomas shows his respect for a famous predecessor by accepting Isidore's definition and divisions; but then Thomas goes on to explain the matter in his own way. All human law is derived from the natural law. *Ius gentium* is human law derived from the natural law by way of deductions; whereas *ius civile* is a further specification and determination of the natural law. Since the *ius gentium* is derived from the natural law by rational deduction, one might truly say that the *ius gentium* is the specifically human or rational natural law *(I-II*, q.95, a.4). Thomas was definitely acquainted with the writings of the older canonists and theologians and frequently tried to reconcile their seemingly opposed views. Thus, even in St. Thomas' writings, there appears some confusion about the definition of natural law and its relationship to other laws.

In general, Thomas' teaching on the natural law is quite clear. The natural law consists in certain very fundamental judgments acquired intuitively and not by deductive reasoning. These are *principia per se nota* which can be reduced to the general principle that good is to be done and evil is to be avoided. The natural law is innate because man learns its first principles from a natural inclination and not from a reasoning process. Thomas compares the first principles of the moral order which are *per se* known to the first principles of the speculative order. From the first principles of the moral order man derives other rules of moral conduct just as other truths are derived from the first principles of the speculative order (*I-II*, q. 94) .

Thomas as well as his predecessors struggled with the problem of the characteristics of the natural law: universality, immutability, and indispensability. I grant that such terminology smacks of legalism, but Thomas was the product of his own times which had been discussing the question in these terms. At least Thomas was aware of the problems concerning the existence of absolute and universal laws of human conduct and in his own way willing to face up to the problem. Perhaps the present discussion about situation ethics is trying to come to grips with the same problem created by the tensions of universal norms and the demands of the concrete situation. The Old Testament itself contained many such problems: Abraham was commanded by God to kill his son; polygamy was allowed; Israelites were told to steal from the Egyptians; Abraham lied to the Egyptians about Sara his wife. In addition the canonists and theologians with their respect for authority had to reconcile the practice of private property with the opinion of Isidore, who maintained that according to the natural law all property should be held in common.[20]

Thomas' concept of universality appears to be much more restricted than the idea of universality often proposed today in the name of Thomas. In nature some things like the sunrise always occur, but other things which usually happen can be impeded by external circumstances and accidents. So in human moral laws some are absolutely universal, such as the primary law of acting according to right reason. Other laws, however, admit of exceptions because of accidental circumstances. It is true that what is owed must be returned, but not if the rightful owner will use the thing to harm others. Since the moral matter is changeable such general laws oblige only *ut in pluribus* (*In III Sent.*, d.37, q.1, a.3, in corp.).

In the *Summa* Thomas delves a little more into the question. Thomas speaks of a twofold universality: a universality concerning the precepts themselves and a universality concerning the knowledge of the precepts. Once man leaves the first principles even in the speculative order, error easily enters into reasoning. In the speculative order the derived principles are always true, even though a particular individual might not realize the truth of such a derived principle. In the practical and moral order, as one descends from the first principles, the principles themselves do not always oblige because of the defectibility of the matter and the other circumstances which may enter into the picture. Thus, Thomas admits that the conclusions of the common principles oblige *ut in pluribus*, but *in paucioribus* they can be defective. Thomas uses just two examples: acting according to reason as an illustration of the common principle and returning what is owed as a conclusion of the first principles. Thomas indicates that whenever deductions occur there is the possibility of an exception; and the more one descends to particulars, the greater the possibility of defections becomes (*I-II*, q.94, a.4).

In discussing the question of the immutability of the natural law Thomas falls back on the same distinction between the first principles and the conclusions of the natural law. The law of nature is completely immutable with regard to the first principles. But the second precepts of the natural law, which are the close conclusions of the first principles, admit some exceptions because of obstacles and impediments (*I-II*, q.94, a.5). Thomas proposed different solutions to explain the various dispensations granted by God in the Old Testament. An act can be opposed to God in two ways: either directly as hatred of God; or indirectly insofar as it

affects other creatures and the harmony existing among creatures. By a miracle God can intervene so that what affects
other creatures does not affect himself. Consequently, God
can intervene and dispense with the obligations of the second table of the decalogue, since they do not affect him immediately *(In I. Sent.,* d.47, a.4).

But Thomas also gives another explanation in the *Sentences* which denies the possibility of a dispensation in the
decalogue. The statements of the decalogue are somewhat
general so that when they are properly understood they do
not admit of exceptions *(In III Sent.,* d.37, a.4, ad 3 um).
Thomas merely follows the two possibilities that are open in
such considerations. If the commandments of the decalogue
are understood in a general sense, they do not admit exceptions. If the commandments are understood more specifically,
they do admit exceptions. In the *Summa,* Thomas flatly
states that the precepts of the decalogue do not allow the
possibility of a dispensation. The biblical exceptions are
not really exceptions because God, the author of life and
the supreme master of all things, is able to dispose of these
as he sees fit *(I-II,* q.100, a.8).

The brief historical survey indicates that before the time
of St. Thomas there was not a coherent philosophical system
with an agreed upon ethical content which was called the
natural law. In Thomas' own synthesis of natural law, he
expressly denies that the natural law is a written code. In
fact, Thomas admits as a principle that once one descends
from the first principles of the natural law which are known
by inclination and not deduction, then the possibility of
defectibility in particular cases becomes a reality. Thomas'
own understanding of the natural law does not seem to
justify the insistence on universally valid, absolute norms of
human behavior in Catholic moral theology. Catholic
thinkers following St. Thomas chronologically did not fol-

low his thinking. A voluntaristic and nominalistic philosophy put much more stress on the will. Outside the limits of Catholic thought, natural law was explained in different ways and used to justify both the divine right of kings and the French revolution.

CONTEMPORARY CATHOLIC THINKERS

The Thomistic revival in the present century has produced some distinguished scholars. The better Thomists take pains to point out that the natural law is not a unified and minute code of ethical actions. Jacques Maritain, for instance, claims that the metaphor of the natural law written on the heart of man has been responsible for the impression that the natural law is a ready-made code rolled up within the conscience of each one of us, which each one of us has only to unroll, and of which all men should naturally have an equal knowledge.[21] John Courtney Murray likewise attacks a legalistic, overrationalistic concept of the natural law.[22] Yves Simon admits that what is wrong by nature can never be rendered right, but he wants to be very cautions before declaring that a particular act is wrong by nature.[23] Speaking of divorce, Simon says: "One thing is sure: complete instability, no restrictions on instability, divorce at will, divorce granted as soon as one partner feels like terminating the marriage is certainly contrary to natural law. Too great a human good would be destroyed by unrestricted instability in the relation of husband and wife. Between some restrictions, enough to give children a chance to be brought up in better than completely casual circumstances, and indissoluble marriage the difference is that between the more necessary and the less necessary."[24] Columba Ryan says about the natural law that its primary injunctions are purely formal and amount to little more than the discrimination between good and evil. According to Ryan, the derivative precepts of the natural law are either so general as to provide little guidance to conduct or else so disputable as to win no general consent.[25]

Other Catholic thinkers today are calling for a more radical revision of the whole concept of natural law. Karl Rahner has observed that natural law should be approached through a transcendental methodology.[26] Kenneth Schmitz has called for the primacy of actual, personal existence over essential, natured individuality and the·consequent relocation and subordination of the natural law.[27] Joseph Arntz maintains that we must realize that natural law is nothing but the truth of living together. "Natural law is itself the primary evidence which unfolds itself constantly, and constantly demands to be translated into concrete human relationships."[28] Robert O. Johann sees natural law in terms of the responsibility of man as a person, open to the Absolute, and called to promote being.[29] John G. Milhaven calls for an epistemology of ethics which gives more importance to empirical evidence.[30] Edward Schillebeeckx admits that modern life accentuates the gap that has always existed between abstract norms and concrete reality. It is the creative function of conscience to close that gap.[31]

In the future, Catholic philosophers and theologians will probably propose more radical explanations of the natural law and even advocate other philosophical systems. Catholic theology, now encouraged by the clear calls for dialogue with modern man made by the Vatican Council, is just beginning to break out of its intellectual ghetto. The text books of moral theology in use in seminaries before Vatican II derived their content, purpose and format from the *Institutiones Theologiae Moralis* of the seventeenth century. They contain, for all practical purposes, no references to other Christian thinkers and to the ethics of contemporary philosophers. The very fact that Catholic life survived for over ten centuries without the benefit of scholastic philosophy shows that Catholic thought is not indissolubly wedded to such a philosophy. The greatness of St. Thomas was his attempt to understand Christianity in the terms that were known in his contemporary society. A true following of St. Thomas demands that contemporary thinkers do for Catholic theology today what Thomas did for it in his day.

The conclusion of this brief historical summary is this: the natural law cannot be the adequate explanation of the generic insistence on universally valid, absolute norms of conduct in Catholic moral theology. The very obvious reason is that for the greater part, if not all, of the Church's existence the natural law has not been a coherent philosophical system with an agreed upon content of ethical norms. Those who espouse the natural law as a method in forming moral judgments are quick to point out that the natural law does not imply the existence of always valid, universal norms of conduct once one descends from the first principles.

NATURAL LAW AND THE FORMATION OF CATHOLIC TEACHING

Now one more point must be made: the Catholic Church and Catholic theology is not irreparably committed to accept the natural law as a coherent system for the understanding of moral conduct. The assertion that the Catholic Church is not wedded to the natural law theory follows from the fact that the natural law has not been a monolithic ethical theory with agreed upon ethical norms throughout the entire history of the Church. A further historical reflection will buttress the assertion. How did the Catholic Church arrive at its moral teaching on most issues such as abortion, birth control, divorce, fornication? I am sure that Clement of Alexandria did not sit down with a team of natural law theoreticians to examine the question of the use of contraception in marital intercourse.[32] The Thomistic natural law synthesis was not even in existence when the Church first formulated its moral teachings in most areas! The natural law theory like any other theory tries to be an explanation of the reality that man knows and experiences. The reality comes first, and the theory has value only to the extent that it corresponds to the reality. Since the term, natural law, was known both to Greek philosophy and Roman law, it is only natural that theologians would use such a concept in trying to explain the teachings of the Church. The vast majority of the moral teachings of the Catholic Church on particular moral problems are not the result of the application of natural law theory to the particular moral point in question.

In the last hundred years the magisterium of the Catholic Church has begun to use the natural law theory in its approach to contemporary moral problems. This usage corresponds with the magisterium's own reemphasis of Thomistic thought.[33] The Church magisterium frequently talks about natural law in its approach to problems of social morality. However, since many non-natural law theoreticians have accepted much of the Catholic teaching on social principles, I do not think that there exists here a rigorous application of natural law theory but rather a general argumentation based on the rights of man and the human person. In fact, the Pastoral Constitution on the Church in the Modern World (*Gaudium et spes*) mentions the term natural law very infrequently.[34]

Perhaps during the present century the one area in which the Church has applied a strict natural law theory to particular moral problems is the area of modern marriage problems and medical ethics (e.g. contraception, sterilization, masturbation, direct abortion, etc.). However, precisely in this area of medical ethics Catholic theologians are questioning some of the conclusions arrived at by the natural law theory as interpreted in the magisterium of the Church.[35] The Catholic Church has never irrevocably committed itself in principle to the natural law theory as the sole means of approaching the solution of moral problems. In practice the vast majority of the Church's moral teachings have not arisen from the application of natural law to particular questions.

The same question can be considered from a more theoretical viewpoint: can the Catholic Church ever commit itself irrevocably to any philosophical system and understanding of man? The sovereign freedom of the Word of God cannot be tied down to any one philosophical understanding of man and reality. Every philosophical theory must be constantly rejudged in the light of the living Word of God. As mentioned earlier, Catholic theology is emerging from an intellectual ghetto. The conciliar stress on the need for dialogue with Christians, non-Christians, and the whole world shows that Catholic thinking can no longer claim a monopoly on the truth. The contemporary emphasis on the pilgrim Church and the increasing awareness of an evolving human existence have made Catholic theology realize that truth is never totally possessed.

The Church was able to exist for the greater part of its history without scholastic thinking, so there can be no absolutely necessary tie between Catholic theology and scholastic thought patterns. Thomas and scholasticism certainly deserve a high place in the history of thought, but in no sense can they constitute the last word in Catholic theological thinking. *De facto*, the Catholic Church has not in the majority of cases used the natural law theory as a method of arriving at a moral judgment about a particular question. *De iure*, the Catholic Church can never irrevocably (I grant that some philosophical theories lend themselves more easily to an interpretation of Catholic thinking, and some theories may be incompatible with the Catholic understanding of the Word of God) commit itself to the natural law theory or any other specific theory as a method for the understanding of Christian behavior. The investigation of the relationship between the natural law theory and the way in which the Catholic Church has arrived at its moral teachings again seems to prove the assertion that the natural law theory cannot be the adequate explanation of the emphasis on absolute norms of behavior which is present in Catholic moral theology.

II. THE TEACHING AUTHORITY OF THE CATHOLIC CHURCH

Does the magisterium or teaching authority of the Roman Catholic Church account for the insistence on absolute norms in moral theology? Obviously there is a connection between the existence of a teaching authority and a more authoritarian teaching on particular issues. Catholic moral theology does believe that the Church helps to interpret what is right and wrong. In the past, the impression has definitely been given that the teaching authority of the Church tends to operate in an a priori and absolutistic way. But, Catholic theology today must begin to reflect more on the way in which the magisterium forms its moral teaching. The recent discussion in the Catholic Church on birth control forces theologians to ask about the way the magisterium or teaching authority functions. The historical fact of change in Church teaching naturally calls for an examination of the way in which the Church does form its moral teaching.

What role does Sacred Scripture play in the formation of Catholic moral teaching? Sacred Scripture is an important guide for the teaching Church. Unfortunately, in the past, Catholic moral theology has not had a scriptural basis and dimension. The Second Vatican Council, however, has reminded theologians that the scriptures are the soul of all theology.[36] The scriptures certainly show the overall context of Christian morality—the covenant of love between God and his people. Man's life and activity must be seen in the light of his existence in the covenant community of salvation. The written word of God insists on the basic attitudes that should characterize Christian life. Faith is the openness to the saving word of God in Christ, and love of neighbor is openness to others. Love of neighbor becomes the infallible sign of Christian existence and is manifested above all in the love of enemies and the willingness to forgive.

Many important themes of the moral life are treated in the scriptures—law, conscience, sin, hope, etc. Some moral questions such as divorce are mentioned in scripture, but the teaching of scripture on these points is not absolutely clear. Many other moral problems confronting the Christian today are not even mentioned in scripture—racial justice, world peace, poverty, euthanasia, questions connected with genetics. The Church even seems to go against the express words of scripture by approving the taking of oaths and the receiving of interest on loans. The teaching authority of the Church must judge all things in the light of the Word of God, but the scriptures themselves do not furnish concrete answers to all the moral problems that are facing modern man.[37] The limits of the moral knowledge derived from scripture are quite apparent, for the scriptures record just one experience of the Christian life in a particular time of history.[38] The teaching authority of the Church must always judge in the light of the Word of God, but the scriptures are not the sole determining element in the teaching authority of the Church.

THE ROLE OF TRADITIONAL TEACHING

Catholic theology has always stressed tradition and the role it plays in forming the teaching of the Church on a particular issue. Theologians today are seeing tradition not as opposed to the scriptures but rather as the living Word of God in time and space. Tradition is most important in forming the moral teaching of the Church, but history teaches that the Church has changed its traditional teaching on certain points.

Usury presents a good example of a change in the teaching of the Church. The prohibition of usury as it existed in 1450 condemned the making of profit from a loan. Certain extrinsic titles would justify compensation; but interest could never be lawfully sought on a loan, nor could the mere risk involved in lending be a just title for compensation or interest. The prohibition of usury was based on some random biblical texts and strongly upheld by such influential Fathers of the Church as Ambrose, Jerome, Augustine, and the more influential of the Greek Fathers. In 1139 the Second Lateran Council condemned "rapacious usury" as detestable and repugnant to divine and human laws. The Third Council of the Lateran (1179) denied Christian burial to manifest usurers. According to the Council of Vienne (1314), a person affirming that the practice of usury is not a sin is to be treated as a heretic. Also a long list of Popes condemned usury. Today, however, Catholic teaching permits the taking of interest on loans and forbids only exorbitant interest.[39]

The question of religious liberty again illustrates the possibility of change in a traditional teaching of the Church. Gregory XVI's encyclical, *Mirari vos*, of August 15, 1832, condemned "the false and absurd maxim, or rather madness, that every individual should be given and guaranteed freedom of conscience, that most contagious of errors, the way to which is opened by the absolute and unfettered freedom of opinion which, to the ruin of Church and State, is spreading everywhere, and which some men, with excessive impudence, have the temerity to describe as beneficial to religion."[40] The encyclical *Quanta Cura* of Pius IX states: "As a result of this utterly false idea of the government of society, they do not hesitate to support the erroneous opinion, than which none is more fatal to the Catholic Church and the salvation of souls, and which our predecessor of happy memory Gregory XVI called a madness, to wit, that freedom of conscience and worship is every man's proper right; that it should be proclaimed and ensured in every well ordered state; and that the citizens have a right and perfect liberty, to voice their opinions, whatever they may be loudly and publicly, in words or through the press, without any limitation by the civil or ecclesiastical authorities."[41]

Among the condemned propositions in the Syllabus of Errors joined to Pius IX's encyclical is the following: "Every man is free to embrace and profess the religion he considers to be the true one by the light of reason."[42] Leo XIII's encyclical *Libertas* condemns religious liberty and the separation of Church and State. "And, first, let us examine that liberty in individuals which is so opposed to the virtue of religion; namely, the liberty of worship, as it is called. . . . Justice therefore forbids, and reason itself forbids, the State to be godless; or to adopt a line of action that would end in godlessness; namely, to treat the various religions (as they call them) alike, and to bestow upon them promiscuously equal rights and privileges."[43]

All these statements must be understood in the light of the historical circumstances of the times, especially the opposition of the Roman Catholic Church to the liberalism of the day. However, there is a great discontinuity between these documents of the official magisterium of the Church and the teaching of the Declaration on Religious Liberty (*Dignitatis humanae personae*) promulgated by the Second Vatican Council. Since the Church has changed its teaching on religious liberty, the mere repetition of the past teaching of the Church is not a sufficient guide for the present teaching Church.

Another example of a change in the traditional teaching of the magisterium concerns the question of the defendant's right to silence. Patrick Granfield has examined the documents of the magisterium and concluded that the privilege against self-incrimination by the defendant was first recognized by the magisterium in the Code of Canon Law (canon 1743), which was promulgated in 1917. Granfield maintains there was no organic development in the magisterium, for as late as 1910 no provision was made for the right to silence. Although the documents involved (a response, a papal bull, a catechism approved by a general council, a statement from a provincial council, a series of papal constitutions, and some procedural norms for the Roman Rota) do not possess the highest magisterial authority, nevertheless, they do form the traditional teaching of the magisterium. However, as early as the seventeenth century English law admitted the right to silence. Obviously, the magisterium changed its traditional teaching in the light of the new developments in civil law and greater awareness of human dignity and rights.[44]

Another topic of discussion among Catholic theologians today is the obligation of the Catholic spouse to raise the children of a mixed marriage in the Catholic faith. Ladislaus Örsy has collected 13 papal documents, 9 documents from the Holy Office, and 8 other documents from the Roman

Curia which teach the divine law obligation of the Catholic spouse to raise the children of a mixed marriage in the Catholic faith. From these documents Örsy concludes that the divine law obligation for the Catholic spouse to care for the Catholic upbringing of the children is a true and immutable Catholic teaching.[45] Örsy himself allows for certain nuances of this conclusion, whereas other theologians even deny the divine law obligation to raise the children of mixed marriages in the Catholic faith.[46]

The Catholic Church always lives in continuity with its past. The Church has learned much in its development, and tradition may well be called the memory of the Church. The Church like every living body or individual must confront the present situation armed with the experience and the knowledge gained from its development. However, the very fact that something was taught at an earlier time in the Church is not a guarantee that the same teaching holds true today. Tradition and scripture are both most important in the formation of the decision of the teaching Church, but they are not adequate criteria in themselves.

What about the use of reason and man's rational faculties in arguing to a particular moral decision? The teaching Church must use all human means to investigate the world and its problems and to apply the gospel message to present day problems. However, history shows that reason alone can come to very different conclusions about particular issues. Theologians cannot always agree on the reasons behind a specific teaching of the magisterium. For example, the teaching magisterium of the Church proposes that masturbation is wrong, but Catholic theologians in history have not been in agreement on the precise reason for the malice of masturbation.[47]

The first part of this essay tried to show that the Catholic Church cannot be committed to any one rational system or explanation of the world. Reason does play an important part in the formulation of the teachings of the magisterium, but reason alone is not an absolute and self-sufficient norm for the teaching Church in considering specific moral problems. How does the teaching authority of the Church form its moral judgments? Scriptures, tradition and reason all play a definite part, but neither singly nor together do they constitute an adequate explanation of the way in which the Church formulates its moral teaching. All Catholics would admit the help of the Holy Spirit in guiding the Church magisterium, but the Spirit does not just produce ready made answers out of a vacuum. I propose that a very important factor in the teaching of the Church is the experience of Christian people. The teaching Church definitely learns from the experience of the living Church.

THE ROLE OF HUMAN EXPERIENCE

The areas in which the Church has changed its moral teachings highlight the importance of the role played by the experience of the Christian people. Different circumstances and a new understanding of money influenced the change in the teaching of the magisterium on interest. But how did the Church become aware of these changing circumstances? I believe that the Church learned from the experience of Christian people and then could look back to rationally justify such a change because of changing circumstances. Any realistic interpretation must admit that the taking of interest did not become right just the moment that the Church said it was allowed. No, the Church authority was merely following the experience of Christian people.

On the question of religious liberty, the Vatican Council expressly admits that the teaching authority of the Church has learned from the experience of Christian people. "A sense of the dignity of the human person has been impressing itself more and more deeply on the consciousness of contemporary man. And the demand is increasingly made that men should act on their own judgment, enjoying and making use of a responsible freedom, not driven by coercion but motivated by a sense of duty. The demand is also made that constitutional limits should be set to the powers of government. . . . This Vatican Synod takes careful note of these desires in the minds of men. It proposed to declare them to be greatly in accord with truth and justice. To this end, it searches into the sacred tradition and doctrine of the Church —the treasury out of which the Church continually brings forth new things which are in harmony with the things that are old. . . ." (Declaration on Religious Freedom, n.1) .

The twentieth century development in the Church's teaching on religious liberty illustrates the truth of the role of experience in the formation of Catholic teaching. The acknowledged architect of the Declaration on Religious Freedom was John Courtney Murray. Murray did not come to his conclusions by an abstract consideration of the nature of Church and State and the dignity of the human person. Murray reflected and rationalized, in the good sense of that term, the experience of the Christian people as found in the American experiment of Church-State relations.[48] Murray shows clearly that theology is a reflection on life; but life and experience came first.The present debate in the Catholic Church on birth control has arisen precisely because of the experience of Christian people. Theologians would never have begun to rethink the whole question unless they had been prodded by the problems raised in the living of marriage in this world. The agonizing reappraisal that the Pope is undertaking illustrates the tension created by a changing experience in the Church. Many Catholic couples have grappled with the same conscience problem in coming to their own personal solutions in the area of responsible parenthood.

Some Catholic theologians might object that the emphasis on the experience of Christian people would destroy the very concept of the Roman Catholic Church and its teaching authority. I do not think so. The renewed Catholic theology of the Church is stressing the fact that the Church is not just the hierarchy and the magisterium but the whole People of God. If the Church is the people of God, then the experience of Christian people would have a part to play in the teaching of the Church. The primary ruler and teacher in the Church is the Holy Spirit, but no one person in the Church has a monopoly on the Holy Spirit. The office of hierarchy is a gift of the Spirit, but the Spirit dwells in the hearts of all the just. The Spirit can also speak in the lives of the Christian people. The teaching Church must always be attuned to the living Word of God and the Spirit no matter where they are found.

Is there truly any need for a teaching authority in the Church if the experience of Christian people is such an important element? Yes, there still remains the need for a teaching authority. One individual can very easily be led astray by his own limitations, prejudice, blindness or sinful egoism. Since the Church is a community, a *koinonia*, the teaching authority of the Church represents the experience of the total community. Only within the total community can one discern the call of the Spirit. The teaching authority of the Church must be willing to test the experience of individuals against the background of the whole community.

Is the teaching authority of the Church reduced to the status of an ecclesiastical George Gallup? No, the teaching authority of the Church does not just count noses on a particular subject. As the community of salvation, the Church owes its existence to the Word of God. During the course of its continued existence the Church has learned much from the accumulated experience of the years. The teaching authority of the Church tests the experience of Christian people in the light of the living Word of God and the memory (tradition) of the Church itself. Consequently, the teaching authority does not merely function by taking a poll of the attitudes of a particular group at a particular time.

The experience of Christian people is not the only element that enters into the way in which the teaching Church comes to its conclusions on particular points. The primary teacher in the Church is the Holy Spirit who speaks in many and diverse ways, one of which is the experience of Christian people. The Church must always teach the central values and attitudes of the Christian life as they are proclaimed in the good news of salvation. The Church at times must also speak about particular issues and problems, but teaching on such matters must be somewhat tentative. The wisdom of the teaching authority of the Church in the past is evident in the fact that the Church has never made an infallible pronouncement on a particular moral issue as such. There are many different ways in which the Church teaches. One might even speak of different magisteria in the Church. The hierarchical teaching magisterium is just one way in which the Church teaches and witnesses to the Word of God in the world of today. However, there are other ways in which the Church carries out its teaching mission.

Even in speaking about particular problems the Church does not depend totally on the experience of Christian people. History, even contemporary history shows that in some areas, such as racial equality, peace, social justice and world poverty, the teaching Church must lead the individual Christians. There is a reciprocity between the living and the teaching Church which defies any neat categories or analysis. However, the experience of sincere Christian people trying to conform to the Spirit remains an important element to be considered by the hierarchical magisterium in the Church.

A proper understanding of the various magisteria and of

the different ways in which the Church teaches indicates that the hierarchical teaching authority as such cannot be the adequate explanation of the generic insistence on absolute norms in Catholic moral theology. The magisterium cannot function merely in an a priori way, but the hierarchical teaching Church also learns from the experience of Christians and all men. Previously, this chapter tried to show that the insistence on absolutes in moral theology is not logically the result of an insistence on the natural law as such. There may be some absolute moral norms about particular moral actions, but our concern has been the overall insistence on absolute norms in moral theology. Neither the natural law nor the teaching authority of the Church is an adequate explanation of the rather generic insistence on absolutes in moral theology.

What is the explanation for the insistence on absolutes in Catholic moral theology? It would be an impossible task to explain adequately the insistence in Catholic theology on universal norms of conduct which are always binding. In the next section I will indicate two factors that I believe have played an important role in the emphasis on absolute norms in moral theology. Since the Catholic Church is not in principle committed to the existence of absolutes in moral theology, and since some of the factors influencing such an emphasis are now changing, the conclusion of this paper is that in the future Catholic moral theology will have to question many of the moral absolutes which heretofore have been upheld.

III. CHANGING THEOLOGICAL AND SOCIOLOGICAL UNDERSTANDINGS OF LIFE IN THE CHURCH

First, an inadequate understanding of the Church, which has characterized Catholic theology since the Reformation, has led to an undue insistence on authority and absolute norms in the life of the Catholic. Reacting against the Protestant concept, Catholic theology stressed the visible aspect of the Church and especially the visible authority in the Church. Pre-Vatican II textbooks on ecclesiology devoted most of their space to the Roman pontiff.[49] Even the role of the bishops and the whole hierarchy did not receive a developed consideration. Only with Vatican II has the notion of the collegiality of the bishops assumed again its proper role in the understanding of ecclesiology.[50] There were nineteenth centuries renewals in a better understanding of ecclesiology, but even after the encyclical *Mystici Corporis*, in 1943, the textbooks still gave a rather one-sided picture of ecclesiology.[51] The Dogmatic Constitution on the Church (*Lumen Gentium*) promulgated by Vatican II now views the Church primarily as the people of God in the covenant community of salvation.

The manuals of moral theology reflected the concept of life within a very authoritarian society that was structured entirely from the top down. Moral theology became a separate branch of learning apart from dogmatic and ascetical theology. Moral theology then assumed a much closer relationship with the science of canon law, so that many considerations in the manuals of moral theology today belong rather to canon law. All morality took on the perspective of relationship to law, for law was seen as the guiding and directing force of all life. The fact that the manuals of moral theology had the primary purpose of training confessors to distinguish between mortal sin and no sin, only heightened the attention given to drawing clear and certain boundary lines between sin and no sin. Moral theology as separated from spiritual theology paid practically no attention to the growth and development of the Christian life—an area in which there is no room for absolute norms which are always binding. Moral theology considered the Christian life primarily in terms of obedience to an elaborate system of laws. The tract on law became one of the primary considerations in moral theology textbooks.[52]

The pre-Vatican II concepts of life, authority and law in the Church do not reflect either the current theological understanding of the Church, or even the circumstances of life in modern secular society. The proliferation of recent studies on law and authority in the Church indicates the changes that are occurring.[53] The Church is no longer equated with its hierarchical structure. Theologians now speak of authority in terms of service of the people of God. Papal infallibility is being discussed, and infallibility is viewed as belonging to the Church itself and exercised in one way through the Roman Pontiff. The Vatican Council renewed the idea of episcopal collegiality and indicated that such collegiality and communitarianism must be found on all levels of life in the Church. The Church no longer appears as an authoritative society completely structured from the top down.

The changing concept of the theology of the Church and authority in the Church also calls for a change in the role of law in the Church.[54] Law in the Church has only an ancillary function. The source of all life in the Church remains the Holy Spirit who dwells in the hearts of all. Law in the Church does not direct all activity but merely serves to create the climate and order in which the community may live under the primary guiding force of the Holy Spirit. Individual responsibility, creativity, and initiative are much more important than mere conformity to an elaborate system of law. The realization of the secondary role of law in the life of the Church will necessarily have repercussions on the emphasis on law in moral theology.

The concept of the Church and its life which was so familiar in Catholic thought before Vatican II resembled very closely the life of the secular society in medieval Europe and in the later period of the monarchies. Such societies were structured from the top down and were relatively static. The life and even the attitudes of the people were completely dependent on the authorities. The famous axiom, *cuius regio eius religio,* indicates that the ruling prince even determined the religion of his subjects. The people were truly subjects and serfs who contributed very little in the way of initiative and creativity.

Catholic teaching on Church and State in the nineteenth century shows the very authoritarian view of society which has pervaded Catholic thinking even to the present times. Pope Leo XIII referred to the people as the untutored multitude.[55] Such people could not decide anything for themselves; they had to be led by their rulers. Since the state directed almost all life in the society, the state had to look out for the religious beliefs of its subjects. The nineteenth century popes with their understanding of society naturally rejected the notion of religious liberty. Only in the last few decades has the Catholic Church accepted a view that realizes the very limited role of government in society. Law, consequently, is not the primary and most important force contributing to the common good of society. Modern society promotes the creativity and initiative of individuals and other groups within society. Law and the state government have the rather limited function of preserving the public order; i.e., of making it possible for the other forces in society to contribute to the common good. Individuals in modern states are citizens and not subjects. Contemporary society is not structured from the top down in an authoritarian way. Men and institutions are given the freedom to develop as best they can for their own good and the good of society.

Catholic moral theology's teaching on probabilism is a good illustration of a teaching that reflects a life situation which is no longer present in the life of the contemporary

Catholic Church. The birth control controversy in the Church has highlighted the inadequacy of the concept of extrinsic probabilism. According to the theory, if a sufficient number of authorities maintain that an opinion favoring freedom from a particular obligation is probable, an individual may follow such an opinion in good conscience. Theologians in the past have debated about how many authorities constitute a probable opinion.[56]

In the matter of birth control, the primary question of priests in the active ministry was whether or not the opinion which says the pill or contraception may be used is probable. One theologian maintained that if the Pope made no authoritative statement within a few months, then the opinion favoring the use of contraception would be probable and could be followed in practice.[57] But how can a certain number of authorities or a certain number of months make something right which was wrong a few months before? (I grant that probabilism does not speak in terms of what is speculatively true but only in terms of practice.)

Probabilism fails precisely because it tries to give a legalistic solution to what should be a prudential decision of conscience made by the individual. Probabilism has a meaning in a society in which people are always looking to the authorities for what they should do. Where people are the unlettered masses with no education and no creative role, a theory appealing to the decision of authorities has intelligibility. But today the situation has changed; conscience must assume its true role in such cases. Conscience must do for the twentieth century Christian what probabilism did for the Catholic in the seventeenth and eighteenth centuries. The prudent Christian will naturally investigate the problem and see what other prudent Christians and experts have to say, but the final decision will rest with the conscience of the individual. Extrinsic probabilism saved the individual from taking the risk involved in a personal decision whenever some doubt existed. Like all legalistic solutions, it is clear, precise, and somewhat easy to apply; but it does not come to grips with the reality of the situation. This is just one example of an inadequacy in moral theology because of an understanding of life and society which no longer corresponds to the reality of life in the Church.

In general, the authorities in the Catholic Church thought they had to direct the entire life of the sheep who were committed to their care. The very word sheep connotes the passive and docile characteristics of the faithful. Even today the hierarchy will frequently talk about the need to protect the simple faithful from the dangers that might beset them. Moral theology has reflected the same concern in its consideration of the scandal of the weak. The scandal of the weak is a reality, but moral theology and the authorities in the Church frequently do not mention the scandal of the strong. Some people today are repulsed by the Catholic Church because its life does not reflect all the demands of human dignity and freedom. The unfreedom in the Church is a scandal to many people of good will.

Today people are speaking of a crisis in obedience and authority in the Catholic Church. The tensions existing about authority in the Church mirror the changing circumstances in which individual responsibility assumes a greater role and authority assumes a lesser role in the life patterns of individual Catholics. Moral theology must also reflect the changing circumstances by placing more emphasis on individual conscience and responsibility with a corresponding deemphasis on the role of laws in the life of the Christian. Moral theology is being forced to reconsider the existence of absolute, universal laws of behavior which are obliging in all circumstances.

An older theology pictured the Church as a perfect society which had all the answers, which were handed down from the authorities of the Church. Triumphalism was one of the most frequent charges made during the Vatican Council. The Church had become smug and triumphal precisely because it thought it had all the answers and did not have to go through the doubts and anxieties of human existence. On the contrary, the Vatican Council in the Dogmatic Constitution on the Church has reiterated time and time again the pilgrim nature of the Church. The Church here on earth is not the Church triumphal; it is not even adequately identified with the kingdom of God. The Church has not yet reached its eschatological perfection, but is striving like Christ to grow in wisdom and age and grace before both God and man. Life in the pilgrim Church is not all structured from the top down.

The concept of the Church as the People of God emphasizes the role that belongs to all Christians in the Church by reason of their baptism. The Vatican Council has renewed the concept of the prophetic office in the Church. (Constitution on the Church, n. 12). In his dealings with his chosen people, God has always raised up prophets to guide his people. The history of renewal in the life of the Church reminds us that renewal frequently comes from underneath and not from the top down.[58] Look at the renewal in the Church that has taken place as a result of the Council. Yes, we are most grateful for Pope John and the Fathers of Vatican II. But there would have been no renewal in the Catholic Church if it had not been for the prophets of the biblical, liturgical, catechetical, and ecumenical movements. Many of these theologians were at one time under a cloud of suspicion, and yet they prepared the way for Vatican II.[59] Like all prophets, they needed the twofold gift which the Lord constantly gives to his prophets—knowledge and the courage to proclaim their message in the face of the established order.

In many other ways the Church has admitted that it does not possess all the answers. The Vatican Council has spoken of the need for dialogue with other Christians, non-Chris-

tians, and the world itself. Dialogue by its very definition assumes that the Church does not have all the answers but is
earnestly searching for the truth in collaboration with all
men of good will. History again records that Roman Catholic theology has relearned many truths in its dialogue with
Protestants—the importance of Scripture, the insistence on
personal commitment, the Church as the people of God, the
ministry as service, etc.

The Church has also learned from the world. The Declaration on Religious Freedom admits that this desire has already been existing in the hearts of men (n. 1). Humanists
and others have been spending themselves even more than
the Church in the interest of racial justice and world peace.
The Roman Catholic Church may rightly be proud of the
teaching in the social encyclicals from Pope Leo XIII to the
present day, but we can never forget that Karl Marx was
there first. Marx realized the injustices involved and tried to
do something constructive for the workers before the Catholic Church realized the problem. The Vatican Council has
sounded the death knell for the picture of the Church as
primarily an authoritarian society structured from the top
down in which the hierarchy, with the protection of the
Holy Spirit, led their children or sheep to eternal perfection.
The Catholic Church will never deny the need and function
of the hierarchy, but for too long the Church was identified
with the hierarchy and little or no role was given to the
people of God.

As the newer theology of the Church makes its impact on
moral theology, more stress will be given to the creativity
and initiative of the Christian people. Christian life will no
longer be seen primarily as obedience to laws and norms. It
would certainly seem that the older view of the Church and
the life of the individual Christian within the Church has
contributed somewhat to the emphasis on absolute norms in
moral theology.

IV. CHANGING THEOLOGICAL METHODOLOGY

A second factor, a question of theological methodology, has influenced the tendency towards absolutes in moral theology. Catholic theologians today speak of a transition from a classicist methodology to a more historically conscious methodology.[60] A classicist methodology tends to be abstract, *a priori*, deductive, and ahistorical. The classicist world view attempts to cut through the accidents of time and history to arrive at the eternal, universal, and unchanging. The universal abstract norms are then applied to the particular situation. The classicist methodology is definitely connected with a Greek way of knowing and thinking. The Platonic notion of a preexisting world of ideas well exemplifies such a methodology. Primary attention is given to substances and essences while the contingent, the particular and the historical are regarded merely as accidents which modify the already constituted reality. The personal, historical, and existential do not receive as much emphasis as they do in modern thought.

An historically conscious methodology proceeds in a different manner. More attention is given to the historical, the contingent, the personal, and existential (without necessarily denying the other aspects of reality). Bernard Lonergan argues for a methodology which "can apprehend mankind as a concrete aggregate developing over time where the locus of development and, so to speak, the synthetic bond is the emergence, expansion, differentiation, dialectic of meaning and of meaningful performance."[61] For Lonergan, meaning is not something fixed, static, and immutable; but shifting, developing, going astray, and capable of redemption.

However, the defenders of the new methodology are quick to point out that such a methodology will not result in a pure subjective ethic, since they too base ethics on reality. However, the concept of reality is more historical and less abstract. The manuals of moral theology definitely reflect a classicist world view. As Catholic theologians begin to employ a more historically minded methodology, questions will naturally be raised about abstract, universal norms of behavior. Perhaps a few illustrations will clarify the use and understanding of a more historically conscious methodology in Catholic moral theology.

John Courtney Murray maintained that the change in the Catholic Church's teaching on religious liberty reflects a change in theological methodology from a classicist to a more historically conscious methodology.[62] The older view of Church-State relations and religious liberty in Catholic theology well illustrates the use of a classicist methodology. The older view started with an abstract view of the perfect society. Then the notion of perfect society was applied to both Church and State. The theory then deduced the relationship which should exist between the two.

However, there were situations in which it was impossible to apply the general principle that the State should recognize and actively support the Catholic Church at the expense of all other Churches. The older theory then distinguished between thesis and hypothesis. The thesis or the ideal always maintains that the State must support the true Church of Christ; but in certain situations the Church may tolerate a system in which the state does not support the Catholic Church but admits a general policy of freedom of conscience and religious liberty. Notice the emphasis on abstract, universal norms which should apply in all circumstances. Even when the historical situation does not permit the application of the general norm, the contrary situation is just tolerated.[63]

The newer view of Church-State does not begin with an *a priori* notion of a perfect society. Murray began from the

concept of the limited state as verified in existing governments today and from the contemporary consciousness of
human dignity and the freedom of conscience in religious
matters. The historical methodology does not demand the
distinction between thesis and hypothesis, between the ideal
and the real.[64] The differing conclusions stem from the different methodologies employed.

The question of the promises in mixed marriages, which
will be developed at greater length in Chapter Seven, also
illustrates the two different methodologies. Most theologians
defend a divine law obligation of the Catholic partner to
raise all the children of a mixed marriage in the Catholic
faith. The argument is based on the truth of the Catholic
Church as the one, true Church of Christ and the obligation
of the Catholic to pass his faith on to all his children. In particular situations the fact that the children will not be raised
in the Catholic faith may be tolerated.[65] The argument is
based on abstract, general truths and obligations. However,
the opinion affirming such an obligation seems to neglect
the very important historical reality of political and even
ecclesiological pluralism as well as the freedom of conscience.

In the light of religious liberty and the reality of ecumenism it seems difficult for me to accept a divine law obligation
to raise all the children of mixed marriages in the Catholic
faith. Notice that the affirmative opinion would be true in
every possible historical situation. It would make no difference if all people freely embraced Catholicism or only a
small minority. The reality of ecumenical ecclesiology today
makes no difference. The freedom of conscience and religious
liberty do not even enter into the principles upon which
the whole solution is based. The defects of a classicist methodology are present in the view affirming a divine law obligation to raise all the children of mixed marriages in the
Catholic faith.

A classicist methodology tends to favor the existence of

absolute, abstract, universal norms in moral theology. The various criticisms recently directed against traditional moral theology seem to center on the fundamental problem of methodology.[66] The classicist methodology tends to be ahistorical, but modern man is very conscious of the importance of history and time. The historical aspect of reality has been submerged in the past. The deductive character of the older methodology tends to emphasize conformity and not creativity. A static world view gives little or no place to growth, development, and change. A Hellenistic view of the universe and nature has a difficulty in explaining the discontinuity in life.

Aristotelian and Thomistic thought do not pay sufficient attention to the individual. For Thomas, man's spiritual individuality is not something positive but negative. Aristotelian philosophy looks to the good of the species and considers the individual good primarily in relationship to the good of the species. Traditional Catholic thought has not given as much place to the individual and the contingent as have more modern philosophies. Catholic moral theology has been accused of naturalism and biologism because of viewing reality in terms of narrow biological laws. Scholastic philosophy has concentrated on substances and essences; whereas modern thought often views reality in terms of the existential and the historical. Modern thought also gives more emphasis to the personal while scholastic philosophy concentrates more on nature.

Absolute certitude is the goal of the classicist methodology, and such certitude is achieved through the knowledge of abstract universals which are always true. Modern sciences never really achieve such certitude, but only a working certitude until they can discover something better. A more historically conscious methodology will not be able to seek the absolute certitude of unchanging universal essences. A change in methodology will have to reflect the best aspects of both approaches, but the greater importance attached to an historically conscious methodology will necessarily mean a lesser emphasis on the existence of absolute norms which are binding in all circumstances.

The traditional Catholic insistence on an intrinsic morality would still be present in a more historically conscious methodology. The terms intrinsically good or intrinsically evil have frequently been understood to refer to actions which are either good or bad in the abstract. However, John Coventry has recently criticized such an understanding of intrinsic morality.[67] Coventry claims that the understanding of intrinsic morality as referring to particular actions in the abstract has resulted from a confusion with the scholastic debate about the possibility of indifferent actions. Intrinsic morality merely means that the act in its total complexity is right or wrong and not right or wrong just because of something extrinsic such as the will of the legislator. In the context of intrinsic morality the object of the human action is not something abstract, but the entire moral complex, the situation, as it is presented to the will. Consequently, such an understanding of intrinsically evil is most compatible with a more historically minded methodology.

All Catholic theology, but especially moral theology, has been at a low point in the past few centuries. The manuals of moral theology merely present the same basic matter as the *Institutiones Theologiae Moralis* of the 17th century which came into existence after the Council of Trent to train confessors as judges in the confessional. For the most part, moral theology has been content to cite the opinions of authorities in the past and occasionally venture a new application. Notice how infrequently, if at all, the manuals of moral theology ever cite an author who is not a Catholic or even a Catholic dogmatic theologian. Moral theology has been divorced not only from the main-stream of secular thinking but even from Catholic dogmatic and ascetical theology.[68]

A defensive and ghetto mentality has prevented moral theology from conducting a dialogue with the thought and life of the modern world. Historical circumstances of the last few centuries have just intensified the defensive and isolated posture of moral theology. The thinking of the modern world was looked upon with suspicion by the Catholic Church, for it seemed to question teachings of the Church. Notice the opposition to Galileo, Darwin, etc. The liberalism of the nineteenth century appeared as a threat to the Church not only in the intellectual sphere but also in the political.[69]

When some Catholics in the past century were beginning to speak of a dialogue or accommodation with modern thought, the Church responded by calling for a renewal of the theology and philosophy of St. Thomas. Dollinger in Germany was trying to break away from older thought patterns, but at that time the Church authorities looked suspiciously upon such moves.[70] The encyclical, *Aeterni Patris* of Leo XIII in 1879, called for a return to the teachings of St. Thomas.[71] Succeeding popes and the Code of Canon Law itself prescribed that philosophy and theology in Catholic schools should be taught according to the reason, doctrine, and principles of the angelic doctor.[72] Excesses with the modernist crisis in the beginning of the present century again emphasized the need to avoid the contemporary thought of the times.[73] Now, however, the Church is talking about the need for dialogue with the modern world and modern thought. In the future Catholic moral theology will be much more open to the philosophical methodologies and thought patterns of the modern world. The emphasis will be away from the classicist world view with its stress on abstract universals.

An excessive rationalism in Catholic theology in the last century has compounded the problems arising from a classicist world view. Other areas of Catholic theology have also experienced an overemphasis on reason and its powers. The First Vatican Council defined that God as the creator can certainly be known from the things of creation through the natural light of human reason (*D.S.* 3001). However, the conciliar section on divine revelation recalled the need for divine revelation so that man in the present condition of the human race can know God with firm certitude and without error (*D.S.* 3005). Nevertheless, the Oath Against Modernism states that God the creator can be known and demonstrated from the things of creation. Although the Oath does not deny the need for revelation as stated in Vatican I, it tends to extol the power of reason by talking in terms of a demonstration and not mentioning any need for revelation (*D.S.* 3538).

Manuals of theology citing Leo XIII and Pius X maintain that it is theologically certain that the existence of God can be scientifically and intellectually demonstrated.[74] Leo XIII even claimed that the State could come to a knowledge of the one true religion since it was so evident.[75] Pius XII in the encyclical *Humani Generis* takes a slightly different tact. He says that although human reason can come to the knowledge of the existence of God, nevertheless, there are many obstacles which prevent such a reasoning process (*D.S.* 3875). The contemporary emphasis on the dialogue with atheism seems to go one step further. Reason for the majority of men does not bring them to a knowledge of God. Catholic theology today stresses the importance and need of faith and is even coming to grips with the problem of crises in faith. Excessive rationalism has also colored most of Catholic apologetics until recently. Reason was thought to prove the existence of God, the fact that Christ was the Son of God, and that the Church is the one true Church of Jesus

Christ. Contemporary apologetics is much different. In general, Catholic theology today is recognizing the excessive rationalism that has been a part of the theology of the manuals.

Moral theology has reflected the general rationalistic tendencies in Catholic theology. Moral theology assumes that reason can solve all the complicated moral problems with clear and definite answers. A typical example of excessive rationalism is the proliferation of books and articles on medical moral problems in the present century. Reason has been invoked to give authoritative and clear cut answers to such delicate moral problems as contraception, sterilization, euthanasia, artificial insemination, seminal analysis, etc. Many theologians are asking questions today precisely about these problems.[76] In the future I do not think that reason can make the apodictic and absolute claims that have been made in the past.

Catholic moral theology is in the process of change and renewal. Moral theology is beginning to dialogue with scripture, dogmatics, and above all with contemporary philosophy. Catholic theology is also aware of an overrationalistic spirit which has characterized the theology manuals before Vatican II. Theological methodology is becoming more historically conscious and departing from a classicist worldview. Such changes, especially in methodology, will influence the insistence on absolute norms in moral theology. I do not categorically conclude that a more historically conscious methodology will deny absolute, universal norms; but such a methodology will not be as favorably disposed to such norms as the older, classicist methodology.

In conclusion, the scope and limits of the present chapter should be underscored. I have not tried to prove that there are no absolute, universally valid norms of conduct in moral theology. For three reasons, such an assertion is beyond the evidence submitted in the chapter. First, there is a problem with the precise meaning of the term, "absolute norms of conduct." Many ethicians would agree on certain very general and vague absolutes. Likewise, even confirmed situationalists will admit very particular, absolute norms of moral conduct with regard to blasphemy, rape, and sexual promiscuity. Second, I have examined only the two factors frequently mentioned as contributing to the Catholic emphasis on absolutes. Third, every particular, absolute norm would have to be considered in itself before one could certainly prove that there are no specific, absolute norms in moral theology.

I have merely tried to prove that neither the natural law nor the teaching authority of the Church, the two reasons frequently proposed, explain the generic insistenc on absolute norms in moral theology. In addition, two other factors, the ecclesiological and sociological understanding of life in the Church as well as theological methodology, which in the past have contributed to the insistence on absolute norms, are now beginning to change. Since the reasons proposed do not explain the generic insistence on absolute norms in moral theology, I conclude that in the future the thrust in moral theology should be away from a generic insistence on such absolute norms. In the light of that thrust, moral theology must reevaluate its teachings on such delicate moral problems as divorce, abortion, masturbation, sterilization, and euthanasia, to mention just some of the problems that moral theology must face. The absolute moral norms calling for reevaluation are those in which the prohibited action is defined in nonmoral terms and sometimes defined merely according to the physical or biological structure of the action.

Notes for Chapter 3

1.
Bernard Häring C.SS.R., *The Law of Christ*, Vol. I (Newman Press, 1961), 501 ff; Häring, *This Time of Salvation* (Herder and Herder, 1966).

2.
Karl Rahner, S.J., *Theological Investigations,* Vol. II (Helicon, 1963) , 212-234.

3.
John C. Bennett, *Christian Ethics and Social Policy* (Charles Scribner's Sons, 1950) , 33-41; Paul L. Lehmann, *Ethics in a Christian Context* (Harper and Row, 1963), 317.

4.
E.g., Joseph Fletcher, *Situation Ethics: The New Morality* (Westminster Press, 1966) , 18-22; Josef Fuchs S.J., *Natural Law* (Sheed and Ward, 1965) , 123-162; also Bennett and Rahner.

5.
John L. Russell S.J., "The Concept of Natural Law," *The Heythrop Journal,* 6 (1965) , 434-438. The historical investigation of the natural law does not pretend to be an original study of the primary sources. I am merely trying to gather together some of the conclusions reached by more recent studies of the historical development of the natural law. For more complete historical studies see Odon Lottin, *Le Droit Natural chez Saint Thomas d'Aquin et ses Prédécesseurs,* 2nd ed. (Charles Beyaert, Bruges, 1931) ; Philippe Delhaye, *Permanence· du Droit Naturel* (Editions Nauwelaerts, 1960) ; Yves R. Simon, *The Tradition of Natural Law* (Fordham U. Press, 1965) , 16-40; Heinrich A. Rommen, *The Natural Law* (B. Herder, 1947) . I have followed Lottin very closely in the exposition of the thinking of St. Thomas.

6.
Joseph Arntz O.P., "Natural Law and its History," *Concilium: Moral Theology,* Vol. 5, n. 1 (May 1965) , 23.

7.
Russell, 438-440.

8.
Gerard Watson, "The Early History of Natural Law," *The Irish Theological Quarterly,* 33 (1966) , 74.

9.
These remarks summarize some of Watson's conclusions and are documented by him, pp. 72-73.

10.
Digest 1, I, tit. 1, 9. The *Corpus Iuris Civile*, the codification of Roman Law by Justinian is divided into the *Digest*, the *Code*, and the *Novellae Constitutiones*.

11.
Digest 1, I, tit. 1, 1, 4.

12.
In IV Sent., d.33, q.1, a.1, ad 4um.

13.
Ibid.; also *I-II*, q.94, a.2.

14.
I-II, q.94, a.4 and 5.

15.
Sancti Isidori Hispalensis Episcopi Etymologiarum, lib. 5, c.5 and 6; in Migne, *P.L.*, Vol. 82, 199, 200.

16.
I-II, q.94, a.4, ad lum; *In IV Sent.*, d.33, q.1, a.1, ad 4um.

17.
Decretum, pars I, d.1.

18.
Lottin, 28-57.

19.
In X Libros Ethicorum ad Nicomachum, lib.5, lectio 12.

20.
Etymologiarum, lib. 5, c. 4. (*P.L.*, Vol. 82, 199). Thomas treats the objection from Isidore in *I-II*, q.94, a.5, ob.3.

21.
Jacques Maritain, *The Rights of Man and Natural Law* (Charles Scribner's Sons, 1943), 62.

22.
John Courtney Murray S.J., *We Hold These Truths* (Sheed and Ward, 1960), 295-336.
23.
Simon, 148.
24.
Simon, 157.
25.
Columba Ryan O.P., "The Traditional Concept of Natural Law: An Investigation," in *Light on the Natural Law*, ed. Illtud Evans O.P., (Helicon, 1965), 33.
26.
Karl Rahner S.J., "Natturrecht," *Lexikon für Theologie und Kirche*, Vol. 7 (Herder Freiburg, 1962), 827, 828.
27.
Kenneth J. Schmitz, "The New Freedom and the Integrity of the Profane," *Proceedings of the Society of Catholic College Teachers of Sacred Doctrine*, 11 (1965), 33.
28.
Joseph Arntz O.P., *Concilium: Moral Theology*, Vol. 5, n. 1 (May 1965), 31.
29.
Robert O. Johann S.J., "Responsible Parenthood: A Philosophical View," *Proceedings of the Twentieth Annual Convention of the Catholic Theological Society of America*, 115-128.
30.
John G. Milhaven S.J., "Towards an Epistemology of Ethics," *Theological Studies*, 27 (1966), 228-241.
31.
E. Schillebeeckx, O.P., *Approches Théologiques II: Dieu et L'Homme* (Editions du Cep, Bruxelles, 1965), 262-269.
32.
John T. Noonan, Jr., *Contraception: A History of Its Treatment by the Catholic Theologians and Canonists* (Harvard University Press, 1965), 57-106.

33.
Leo XIII in his encyclical letter, *Aeterni Patris* of Aug. 4, 1879, *Acta Sanctae Sedis*, 11 (1878-9), 98 ff., prescribed the restoration in Catholic schools of Christian philosophy in the spirit of St. Thomas Aquinas. For subsequent papal directives on following the philosophy and theology of St. Thomas, see Pius X, *Doctoris Angelici* (*Motu Proprio*), *Acta Apostolicae Sedis*, 6 (1914), 384 ff.; Pius XI, *Officiorum Omnium* (Encyclical letter), *A.A.S.*, 14 (1922), 449 ff.; Pius XI, *Studiorum Ducem* (Encyclical Letter), *A.A.S.*, 15 (1923), 323 ff.; various allocutiòns of Pius XII, *A.A.S.*, 31 (1939), 246 ff.; 38 (1946), 387 ff.; 45 (1953), 684 ff. According to Canon 1366 of the Code of Canon Law promulgated in 1917, rational philosophy and theology should be taught *"ad Angelici Doctrois rationem, doctrina, et principia. . . ."* *Acta Apostolicae Sedis* will be indicated in the future by *A.A.S.*
34.
J. Jullien, "Nature et culture: Droit naturel ou droit culturel?" *Supplément de la Vie Spirituelle*, 78 (1966), 449. Jullien claims that the Pastoral Constitution on the Church in the Modern World never mentions the term, natural law (*droit naturel*). However, the term is mentioned in n. 74 and n. 79.
35.
Archbishop Denis E. Hurley, "A New Moral Principle," *The Furrow*, 17 (1966), 619-622.
36.
Dogmatic Constitution on Divine Revelation (*Dei Verbum*), n. 24.
37.
E. Hamel S.I., "L'usage de l'Écrite Sainte en théologie morale," *Gregorianum*, 47 (1966), 53-85.
38.
For the use of scripture as a source of knowledge, see Eugene Fontinell, "Reflections on Faith and Metaphysics," *Cross Currents*, 16 (1966), 37-39.

120   *A New Look at Christian Morality*

39.
John T. Noonan, Jr., *The Scholastic Analysis of Usury* (Harvard University Press, 1957). For a brief summary of the teaching of the magisterium on usury and interest, see Noonan, "Authority, Usury, and Contraception," *Cross Currents*, 16 (1966), 55-79.
40.
Acta Gregorii XVI, 1, 172.
41.
Acta Sanctae Sedis, 3 (1867), 162.
42.
Acta Sanctae Sedis, 3 (1867), 170, n. 15.
43.
Acta Leonis XIII, 8 (1888), 229, 231. An English translation may be found in *The Church Speaks to the Modern World: The Social Teaching of Leo XIII*, ed. Etienne Gilson (Image Books, 1954), pp. 70-71, n. 19,21. The English translations are from Gilson.
44.
Patrick Granfield O.S.B., "The Right to Silence: Magisterial Development," *Theological Studies*, 27 (1966), 401-420.
45.
Ladislaus Örsy S.I., "Documenta selecta de educatione religiosa prolis ex matrimonio mixto natae," *Periodica de Re Morali, Canonica, Liturgica*, 53 (1964), 267-284.
46.
Ladislaus Örsy S.I., "The Religious Education of Children Born from Mixed Marriages," *Gregorianum*, 45 (1964), 739-760; Charles E. Curran, *Christian Morality Today* (Fides, 1966), pp. 93-105; and especially Chapter Seven of this volume.
47.
V. Vangheluwe, "De Intrinseca et Gravi Malitia Pollutionis," *Collationes Brugenses*, 48 (1952), 108-115.
48.
John Courtney Murray S.J., *The Problem of Religious Freedom* (Newman Press, 1965). This monograph originally appeared in *Theological Studies*, 25 (1964), 503-575. Also

Murray, "The Declaration on Religious Liberty," *Concilium: Moral Theology*, vol. 5, n. 2 (May 1966), 310.
49.
E.g., Ioachim Salaverri S̈.I., *Sacrae Theologiae Summae I: De Ecclesia Christi* (Biblioteca de Autores Christianos, Madrid, 1955), 497-988.
50.
Dogmatic Constitution on the Church (Lumen Gentium), Chapter III.
51.
Peter Riga, "The Ecclesiology of Johann Adam Möhler," *Theological Studies*, 22 (1961), 563-587.
52.
E.g., N. Noldin S.J., A. Schmitt S.J., G. Heinzel S.J., *Summa Theologiae Moralis I: De Principibus*, 33rd ed. (Oeniponte, Rauch, 1960), contains six different "books"—the last end of man, human actions, laws, conscience, virtues, sins. The longest of the six books is the one on law.
53.
Problems of Authority, ed. John M. Todd (Helicon, 1962); Yves Congar, O.P., *Power and Poverty in the Church* (Helicon, 1964); John L. McKenzie S.J., *Authority in the Church* (Sheed and Ward, 1966).
54.
The proceedings of a recent seminar on "The Role of Law in the Church," sponsored by the Canon Law Society of America, have been published by Helicon Press under the title *Law for Liberty: The Role of Law in the Church Today*, ed. James E. Biechler.
55.
Leo XIII, *Libertas Praestantissimum*, n. 23. Earlier (n.19) the Pope spoke of freedom of worship as being opposed to the virtue of religion. *Acta Leonis XIII*, 8 (1888), 233.
56.
Noldin, n. 238.
57.
Richard A. McCormick S.J., "Notes on Moral Theology," *Theological Studies*, 26 (1965), 646.

58.
Karl Rahner S.J., *The Dynamic Element in the Church* (Herder and Herder, 1964).
59.
Yves M. J. Congar O.P., "The Need for Patience," *Continium*, 2 (1965), 684-693.
60.
Murray, *Concilium: Moral Theology*, vol. 5, n. 2 (May 1966), 7-10; "The Transition from a Classicist World-View to Historical Mindedness," a paper presented by Rev. Bernard Lonergan S.J., to the seminar on the "Role of Law in the Church." The essay is published in *Law for Liberty*. Although some philosophers and theologians who argue for a more historically conscious methodology would reject the teachings of St. Thomas, Lonergan and others claim to be in the tradition of St. Thomas. Many of the distortions in the classicist approach come from his commentators and not from Thomas himself.
61.
Lonergan, "The Transition from a Classicist World-View to Historical Mindedness."
62.
Murray, *Concilium: Moral Theology*, vol. 5, n. 2 (May 1966), 7.
63.
Murray, *The Problem of Religious Freedom*, 7-17.
64.
Murray, *The Problem of Religious Freedom*, 17-45.
65.
See notes 45 and 46.
66.
Charles E. Curran, *Christian Morality Today: The Renewal of Moral Theology* (Fides Publishers, 1966), 127-133.
67.
John Coventry S.J., "Christian Conscience," *The Heythrop Journal*, 7 (1966), 152-153.

68.
Bernard Häring C.SS.R., *The Law of Christ*, Vol. 1 (Newman Press, 1961), 3-33.
69.
R. Aubert, *Le pontificat de Pie IX* (Blond & Gay, Paris, 1952), 224-261.
70.
Aubert, 240-242; 259-260.
71.
H. Denzinger S.J., A. Schönmetzer S.J., *Enchiridion Symbolorum Definitionum et Declarationum de Rebus Fidei et Morum*, 32nd ed. (Herder Freiburg, 1963), n. 3135-3140. Hereafter cited as *D.S.*
72.
The pertinent references are given in note 33.
73.
John Wm. Padberg, "The Modernist Crisis Half a Century Later," *Proceedings of the Twentieth Annual Convention of the Catholic Theological Society of America* (1965), 51-66.
74.
Iosephus M. Dalmau S.I., *Sacrae Theologiae Summa II: De Deo Uno et Trino* (Biblioteca de Autores Cristianos, 1955), Thesis 2: Existentia Deo potest scientifice et intellectualiter demonstrari, 27 ff.
75.
"And if it be asked which of the many conflicting religions it is necessary to admit, reason and the natural law unhesitatingly tell us to practice that one which God enjoins, and which men can easily recognize by certain exterior notes, whereby Divine Providence has willed that it should be distinguished because, in a matter of such moment, the most terrible loss would be the consequence of error." *Libertas Praestantissimum, Acta Leonis XIII*, 8 (1888), 230; Gilson, p. 72, n. 20.
76.
Hurley, *The Furrow*, 17 (1966), 619-623; Curran, 128, 129.

Church Law
and Conscience

Chapter Four

The consideration of the relationship between Church law and conscience will embrace three areas of investigation: (1) the concept of positive law in the Church; (2) the relationship between law and sin; (3) the observance of positive law in the life of the Christian. In the following discussion Church law or canon law always refers to the purely positive laws of the Roman Catholic Church and not to the restatement of other obligations.

THE CONCEPT OF POSITIVE LAW IN THE CHURCH

In his epistle to the Romans, Paul explains the freedom of the Christian as a freedom from sin, death, and the law. St. Paul does not merely say that the Christian is freed from the ceremonial and juridical aspects of the law. Paul apparently uses law to mean, in this particular case, the entire Mosaic law insofar as the Mosaic law is an example of a general economy of law. The Christian is freed from living under an economy of law in the sense that his salvation would depend upon his observance of certain laws or precepts. Salvation comes through faith in Christ Jesus. Freedom from law, however, does not mean that the Christian can now do whatever he pleases. Through the gift of the Spirit the Christian has received the new life in Christ Jesus. He must now produce in his life the fruits of the Spirit and walk according to the Spirit. The primary law for the Christian is the Spirit who dwells in the hearts of the just. The law of the Spirit is a law of freedom precisely because its demands are not imposed upon man from outside. The love of God is poured into our hearts by the Holy Spirit. The Spirit gives us the new heart which then directs all the activities of the Christian. The Spirit becomes the vital principle of Christian life and activity. The primary law for the Christian is "the law of the Spirit giving life in Christ Jesus" (Rom 8:2) .

Since the primary law of the new covenant is the Spirit who dwells in the hearts of the just, canon law and Church law necessarily assume a secondary and ancillary role. Too often in the past, the prevailing attitude has given too much importance to the role of positive law in the life of the Church. Canonical legislation should not occupy the primary role in the living of the Christian life. In discussions about eliminating Friday abstinence, some people object that the changes are doing away with all mortification in Christian life. Such objections betray a mentality that equates the Christian life with the observance of the positive laws of the Church. The greatest mortification remains always the attempt to live out the Paschal Mystery in everyday life. The attitude of some Catholics in the past implied that laws make people holy. A proliferation of laws in many religious communities seems to bear out that understanding of law. However, the notion that more and better laws make people holy is totally inadequate. St. Paul reminds us that laws only provoke more transgressions. History indicates that positive laws have come into existence when the ebb of Christian life was already low. As long as Christians maintained a real understanding of the Eucharist, there was no need to make a law about receiving communion once a year. Positive laws are neither the source of Christian life nor an adequate sign of vitality in the Christian community.

However, there is a need for positive law in the Church. Since the Church strives to be a community of love in this world, positive law will always have its place in the life of that community. Although the community owes its continued existence primarily to the Spirit, positive law plays a secondary role in the life of the Church. Positive law is a necessity in any community for the well being of the community itself and the individuals who comprise the community. Life in a community demands a certain amount of order which positive law seeks to obtain. If just two or three people are living together, they can decide among themselves what they intend to do; but when there is a large community, there is need for established order within which the community lives and functions.

The positive law of the Church, like all other externals in the Church, has a sacramental character. The law must be a sign of the inner reality of the Church, which is above all the community of love. The whole purpose of the law of the Church must be to build up the Body of Christ in truth and love. Canon law should strive to create the climate in which the Church and its individual members can better respond to the call of the Spirit.

Law in the Church cannot be considered in exactly the same way as law in any other society, for the Church is a unique community. Naturally, there are many analogies between the Church and other communities, but the law of the

Church must always manifest the unique character of the community of salvation. Church law has the somewhat negative function of preserving the necessary order in the Church so that the community and individuals can best accomplish their God-given destiny. At the same time Church law should also exercise a more positive function in pointing out some of the demands of the Spirit for the community and the individual Christian. In its more positive and even creative function, Church law must be careful not to stifle the freedom which it is trying to promote. Unfortunately, in the past positive law played too dominant a role and stifled rather than stimulated the life of the Church.

Roman Catholic theological tradition has embraced two divergent understandings of positive law. The Thomistic concept defines law as the *rationis ordinatio ad bonum commune, ab eo qui curam communitatis habet, promulgata* (*I.II.*q.91,a.4) . In the Thomistic tradition law is primarily an ordering of reason. There is another school which is more voluntaristic and is represented by Scotus and Suarez. In the voluntaristic concept, law is primarily an act of the will of the legislator. The speculative differences about the concept of law have very practical consequences. In a Thomistic understanding, something is commanded because it is good in itself. In the voluntaristic viewpoint, something is good precisely because it is commanded.

The first practical consequence concerns the obliging force of law. A voluntaristic concept derives the obliging force of law primarily from the will of the legislator. The Thomistic understanding of law derives the moral obligation of law from the ordering to the common good of the society. Notice the realism present in the Thomistic approach. The law must correspond to the reality of the situation and not just to the will of the legislator.

A second practical consequence concerns the role and function of the legislator himself. In a voluntaristic understanding the will of the legislator is supreme. Everything depends on the will of the legislator. Such a concept of positive law certainly represented the sociological situation of feudal and monarchical society. The legislator was supreme, and his will determined what was to happen in the area in which he ruled. As an example, note the axiom—*cuius regio, eius religio.* In a more Thomistic interpretation, the will of the legislator is not the last word. The legislator must conform himself to the needs of the society here and now. In my application of the Thomistic teaching today, I am not understanding the *ordinatio rationis* in the same sense as St. Thomas did. Nor did St. Thomas see the role of the legislator in the same way that I am envisioning the legislator today. However, Thomas has established the basic principle of realism—the law must reflect the needs of the community here and now. Consequently, the legislator is not the last word. The legislator must conform himself to the needs of the community.

An examination of the old axiom—"the will of the superior is the will of God"—will help focus the conflicting viewpoints. A voluntaristic understanding of law can accept that axiom as being true. However, a more realistic understanding must reject such an axiom. The will of the superior is not the will of God. I am not denying that the superior in some way takes the place of God. But the superior takes the place of God not in his function of willing a law, but in his function of ordering for the needs of the community. The sad lessons of history remind us that we cannot identify the will of the superior with the will of God.

The role of the legislator or superior in a realistic understanding of law corresponds very well with the biblical description of authority. Jesus emphasized the difference between the rulers of this world and his own apostles. The rulers of this world lord it over their subjects and make all men feel the weight of their authority. But, whoever has authority among the apostles must become the servant and the slave of all, for Christ himself came not to be served but to serve and give his life as a ransom for many (Mark 10:42-45). The legislator does not rule supreme because his law is the last word on the subject. Rather, as the humble servant of the community, the legislator tries to unite the service and love of all the members so they can work together for their own fulfillment and the fulfillment of the whole community.

The legislator in the Church must always see his role as the servant of the community trying to order the life of the community according to its own needs and purposes. In addition, the legislator in the Church is the servant of the Spirit. The Spirit and the law of the Spirit must always remain supreme in the Church. The legislator must always conform himself to the call of the Spirit. The legislator can never proceed arbitrarily as if his will makes something right or wrong. The legislator rather must conform his will and his laws to the call of the Spirit and the needs of the community. The legislator in the Church, as well as all authority in the Church, remains always the servant of the Spirit and the servant of the community. The servant role of the legislator corresponds with the necessary but secondary role of law in the life of the Church. A Thomistic or realistic understanding of law reemphasizes the biblical notion of law and authority in the Church.

THE RELATIONSHIP BETWEEN LAW AND SIN

Can Church law bind under penalty of mortal sin? On this specific point, the Code of Canon Law has been much more accurate than the teaching of some theologians. Actually, the Code of Canon Law is very discreet and does not talk in terms of sin. But too frequently, on a popular level, one hears, for example, not simply that it is a "grave matter" but that all Catholics are obliged under pain of mortal sin to participate in the Eucharist on Sunday. Sin, however, should never be conceived as a penalty for the violation of Church law. Sin is not primarily a penalty or a punishment. Rather, sin is the reality of man's breaking his relationship of love with God. If man has not broken his relationship with God, the Church cannot say that he did. The Church has no right to use sin as a penalty for its own laws.

The idea of sin as a penalty for the infringement of Church laws probably owes its origins to an overly slavish imitation of an earlier secular society and authority. Secular society uses penalties as threats to bring about observance of the law. The Church in the past has succumbed to the temptation to use sin as a penalty and a threat to insure the observance of a Church law. But in so doing, the Church has acted more like secular society and not in accord with her own true nature. I am not saying that Church law cannot deal with sanctions, but purely Church law can never use sin as a penalty or a punishment. Sin is the reality of man's breaking his relationship with God and is not just an extrinsic penalty which the Church can attach to particular actions.

Can mere positive Church law propose that certain actions are mortal sins? For example, it is a mortal sin to miss the breviary or it is a mortal sin to miss Mass on Sunday. Church law should not speak in terms of sin. Church law must consider the need for certain actions to be done or others to be avoided. The commission of certain actions or the omission of others might be a sin for this particular person here and now, but the Church cannot speak about the action itself as being a sin. The manuals of moral theology mention three conditions that are required for mortal sin: (1) grave matter, (2) advertence to the gravity of the matter, and (3) perfect consent of the will. (Personally I believe that mortal sin ultimately consists in the involvement of the subject in a particular action. Mortal sin involves a fundamental option of the person in the particular choice which he makes. The three conditions mentioned above for mortal sin are presumptive guidelines and not the ultimate explanation of mortal sin.) Church law only speaks about the matter itself and does not consider advertence or consent. Consequently, Church law cannot speak in terms of sin. Church law can only speak about the greater or lesser importance of a particular action for the life of the community. And this is precisely what the Code of Canon Law does. It speaks about the relative importance of a particular matter in the life of the community and the individual. The expressions, "grave matter" or "light matter", refer precisely to the greater or lesser importance which the Church attaches to a particular action.

However, the Church in this time of renewal must ask if any one particular action is really that important a matter. For example, it was commonly taught by theologians that it was grave matter to omit even a small hour of the breviary. Any realistic understanding must conclude that missing the recitation of the breviary is not an important matter. There are so many important matters in the world today that the Church exposes herself to ridicule by maintaining that such things are that important. In considering the importance attached to praying the breviary daily, one can see quite clearly at work the attitude that has used sin or the threat of sin to bring about compliance with the law. But the Church can never use sin as a penalty or a threatened penalty. Participation in the Eucharistic banquet is certainly an important matter for the Christian; but I think that the importance of participation every single Sunday has been exaggerated by most theologians and canonists.

By speaking merely in terms of the greater or lesser importance of certain actions, the Church can do much in the proper formation of Christian consciences. The final judgment and application in a particular situation will be left up to the individual. Unfortunately, in the past the observance of the laws of the Church has become the infallible criterion of Christian life for many Catholics. Legalism has had an adverse effect not only on the formation of individual consciences but also on the attitude of the Church as a whole. Legalism easily leads to a mediocrity that stifles all creativity and initiative.

The overemphasis on the law serves as a crutch which saves the teaching Church from exerting all its necessary efforts. It is so much easier to say that missing Mass on Sunday is a mortal sin than it is to show by our celebration that we believe the Eucharist to be an important matter in the life of the Christian. The temptation to become administrators and just cite the law has often usurped the teaching office and function in the Church. Legalism also leads to a smugness, a sterility, and an unwillingness to see the need for necessary change. I believe that for too long pastors and teachers have relied on the Sunday obligation to coerce people to "hear Mass". I am convinced that if we had to meet open competition in presenting the meaning of the Eucharist to Christian people somewhat as a soap commercial on T.V. has to meet competition openly, we would not have left our presentation completely unchanged for the past four centuries. How long would an announcer last in the competitive field of T.V. advertising if he spoke in a foreign language, mumbled his lines, and kept his back turned to the people? Legalism has made us all a bit lazy. Yes, law will always be necessary in the Church, but its function is always secondary and dependent on the law of the Spirit.

THE OBSERVANCE OF POSITIVE LAW IN THE LIFE OF THE CHRISTIAN

In any society there will be a tension between the laws of the community and the rights of the individual. The Church experiences these tensions not only because it is a society like others but even because of its own peculiar nature. The fundamental law for the Christian and for the Church is the law of the Spirit, which is primarily an internal law. There is a need for external law in the Church, but this external law must be in conformity with the demands of the internal law. Obviously, here is the first source of tension in the life of the Church. The external law might not always correspond to the demands of the Spirit here and now. The external law of the Church might say that religious vows are by their very nature permanent, but for the good of an individual here and now such vows may become a positive hindrance. The Church law prescribes a certain formulary of prayers for her religious and clerics in major orders. However, perhaps the prescribed prayer does not meet the needs of a particular individual.

A second source of tension comes from the unique nature of the Church itself as the pilgrim Church. Precisely because the Church has not yet arrived at its final goal and perfection, there will always be the possibility of conflicting demands. The pilgrim Church must constantly change its laws, but actual change might lag behind the changes that have already occurred in the life of the community itself. For example, today there are very few who abide by the canonical restrictions on the buying and selling of church property.

A third source of tension is common to all societies and communities—the tension between the individual and the society itself. Such a tension exists because the individual is not completely subordinated to the society. Totalitarianism or collectivism demands the total subordination of the individual to society. On the other hand, only anarchy would maintain that the individual is completely independent of the demands of society. Society and the individual are going to exist in a constant state of tension precisely because they are neither totally independent nor totally dependent on one another. A true Christian communitarianism should avoid the extremes of collectivism, on the one hand, and, on the other hand, anarchy. In this tension one finds the theological defense of so-called civil disobedience. When the law interferes with the inalienable rights of individuals, then it can no longer be a binding law.

A fourth source of tension is the very nature of positive law itself. Most Catholic theologians teach with St. Thomas that positive law admits exceptions. Positive law obliges *ut in pluribus*. Since positive law is not based on immutable essences but on changing circumstances, the legislator cannot possibly foresee all the different circumstances that might arise in a particular case. There are times when the letter of the law can become an injustice for an individual. In fact, the very imperfection of positive law appears more readily in the Church than it does in many secular societies and states. Nations are more homogeneous groupings of people than the Church. For example, here in the United States, people enjoy the same type of climate, the same basic culture of a technological civilization, a high degree of education, a common history and heritage. Consider the difficulties involved in framing laws for people living all over the globe, in completely different climates, with opposing cultural formations, with no common heritage, with differing languages and customs. A law enacted for a greater number of people living in very disparate circumstances will necessarily admit more exceptions than a law made for a more homogeneous grouping of people. Any revision of Canon Law must take into account the principle of subsidiarity, but existing legislation which tries to be at one and the same time rather minute and adaptable for all people in the Church must admit of a greater number of exceptions than most existing civil laws.

A fifth source of tension comes from the possibility of human error. Our nation has already admitted that prohibition was a mistake and has repealed the law. Is it possible for the Church with the guidance of the Holy Spirit to be led astray by human error? The Apostolic Constitution, *Veterum Sapientia*, is an excellent example of error on the part of the lawmaker in the Church.

The rapidly changing sociological conditions of modern life merely accentuate the inherent tensions in human law, and consequently, in Church law. In rather stable and immobile times, the tensions might not be apparent. However, the tensions existing in Church law today are also aggravated by a problem peculiar to the life of the Church here and now. The law of the Church as it exists in the Code of Canon Law reflects a period of life, both in the Church and in secular society, which gave much more emphasis to the place of law in the life of the person. Even in considerations of secular society many Catholic theoreticians have not realized the shrinking place that law occupies in civil society. Catholic theologians frequently speak of law as existing for the common good of society. However, it seems that the function of law is geared for the public order, which is much more limited than the concept of the common good.

There are many and different groups within society which must work for the common good. Law today does not have the function of controlling and directing most of the life within the community. Rather, the role of law is limited to assuring that all these other smaller societies and institutions can make their contribution towards the common good. The role and place of law in the secular society today is much less than it was in medieval society. The recent Church-State and religious liberty controversies point up the changed role of law and government in modern society. Law provides the framework within which the individuals and the different institutions within society can make their contribution for the common good. Perhaps the predominant role given to law in the life of the Church reflected the secular societies of the medieval period; but society and the role of law in society have greatly changed since that time.

The biblical teaching on law and the contemporary theological understanding of the Church show that law has only an ancillary role in the life of the Church. However, the Church is currently living under a legislative system which reflects an epoch in which law played a more predominant role. As the emphasis swings from conformity to creativity, the tensions created by law in the Church are only going to increase. The present Code of Canon Law does not reflect the current theological understanding of the role of law in the Church; nor does it reflect the role of law in modern civil societies.

However, moral theology has always taught that there are built-in safeguards to deal with the possible sources of tension relating to law in the Church. Manuals of moral theology spend a great number of pages discussing excusing causes, dispensations, privileges, etc. However, there is one built-in safeguard which requires greater emphasis today— *epikeia*.

Catholic moral teaching also embraces two different notions of *epikeia*. Most manuals of theology actually adopt a very restricted and Suarezian understanding of *epikeia*. *Epikeia* has usually been surrounded with many precautions and safeguards. If the obliging force of law comes from the will of the legislator, then *epikeia* must be seen in terms of the will of the legislator. In any given situation an individual must have recourse to the will of the legislator to determine if the particular law is still obliging. If in an individual situation it is impossible to approach the legislator, then the individual may act according to the presumed will of the legislator. *Epikeia* is looked upon with some suspicion because it goes against the letter of the law.

The Thomistic teaching on *epikeia* is quite different. Thomas makes the flat assertion that *epikeia* is a virtue (*II. II*. q. 120. a.1.). Despite the objections that *epikeia* might foment anarchy, cause dissensions, or harm the common good, Thomas still asserts that *epikeia* is a virtue. The Thomistic teaching maintains that *epikeia* is a part of the virtue of justice precisely because of the inherent imperfections of human law. *Epikeia* for Thomas is not a lazy attempt to escape from certain obligations, but rather *epikeia* is the response to a higher law, the law of justice. *Epikeia* has been called the crown of legal justice and the virtue of the spirit of the law. For the Christian, *epikeia* cannot be merely the wish to free oneself from a particular obligation, but rather *epikeia* must be a demand of the higher law—the law of the Spirit.

The question naturally arises about the need to have recourse to the legislator before using *epikeia*. A voluntaristic notion of law and *epikeia* stresses the need to have recourse to the will of the legislator. Since in this view the obligation stems from the will of the legislator, the individual should have recourse to the will of the legislator to see if the obligation is still existing. *Per se* the Thomistic notion of *epikeia* does not demand recourse to the legislator. A realistic interpretation of law puts the obliging force of law in the ordering for the common good (better: the public order). If the law does not contribute to the common good in these circumstances, then it no longer obliges. Thomas' own teaching on *epikeia* does at times demand the need for the determination of the ruler. Thomas maintains that in doubtful matters there is need for interpretation, and in these cases it is not permitted to go against the letter of the law without the determination of the ruler (*principis*). But in obvious cases, there is no need for interpretation, but only for execution.

I believe that the Thomistic understanding of *epikeia* is valid today with some adjustments because of the changed sociological circumstances. It is important to realize in the Thomistic understanding that *per se epikeia* does not require recourse to the will of the legislator. Thomas demands recourse only for interpretation in doubtful cases. I contend that today even in doubtful cases the interpretation of the legislator is not the last word. Certainly, the presumption must always stand for the justice of the particular law, but the presumption must cede to the truth in particular cases. The role of the individual in society has changed greatly since Thomas' time. Today both in the Church and in secular society the stress is on the freedom and responsibility of the individual. People in secular society are citizens and not subjects. The whole structure of modern society depends upon the creative contributions of individuals and institutions within society. Law contributes only a small part to the common good of society. Thomas knows only a society which is structured from the top down—everything must come from the command and word of the ruler. (The very word *princeps* used by Thomas indicates that he is not talking about the same type of society that we know.) Less than a century ago, Pope Leo XIII could refer to subjects as the unlettered masses. This is not true in modern society. Society has changed, and the role of the legislator and the individual member in society has changed since the thirteenth century. Consequently, even for interpretation, recourse to the legislator is not required. In many circumstances today such recourse would be virtually impossible.

Our present understanding of law in the Church also shows that interpretation does not demand recourse to the legislator with the final outcome depending on his judgment. The primary law for the Christian is the law of the Spirit. Every other law is secondary. The Christian is entrusted by God with the responsibility of listening to the voice of the Spirit. External law is necessary, the presumption is always with the legislator; but the ultimate decision in the particular case rests with the individual himself.

The twelfth chapter of Matthew's gospel offers a good illustration of the virtue of *epikeia*. Christ himself justifies the breaking of the letter of the Sabbath law to heal the man with a withered arm. Christ reminds his hearers that they too would break the letter of the law even to free a sheep that may have fallen into a ditch. Notice that no recourse for interpretation is required in these cases. Christ also recalls the story from the Old Testament in which David and his men ate the sacred loaves which according to the law could be eaten only by the priests. In cases of emergency, obviously the letter of the law is no longer binding.

The objection immediately comes to mind—*epikeia* ultimately leads to anarchy. By stressing the need for the individual to make the final decision, *epikeia* results in pure subjectivism and anarchy. However, the objection is not valid if one has a proper understanding of the virtue of *epikeia*. *Epikeia* does require that ultimate responsibility rests with the individual, but such a concept does not lead to anarchy.

First, *epikeia* is a part of the virtue of justice. *Epikeia* does not mean license and the possibility of following personal whims and selfishness. Some authors have called *epikeia* the crown of justice, for at times a literal interpretation of the law would violate justice.

Second, *epikeia* is closely connected with the virtue of prudence. Prudence is probably the most forgotten virtue in the manuals of moral theology. Prudence is basically an art. No one can really teach prudence to another, and yet all have an obligation to learn prudence in their daily life. In the past, moral theology has tried to do away with the virtue of prudence by an exaggerated casuistry that tried to solve in advance every conceivable type of problem. Today, many people are calling for prudence. However, prudence, according to St. Thomas, is always a virtue of action. Prudence does not mean an unwillingness to act, rather prudence is the virtue that is present in every risk and decision in the Christian life.

Third, *epikeia* is always a demand of the higher law, the law of the Spirit. *Epikeia* is not a mere sneaking out from some positive obligation. The law of the Spirit is the ultimate criterion in the use of *epikeia*. The individual is trying his best to conform himself to the call of the Spirit in a particular situation. Openness to the Spirit is completely incompatible with irresponsibility and a selfish seeking of the easiest way out in a given situation. Contemporary theology needs to develop the treatise on the rules for the discretion of spirits. The discernment of the Spirit is a most important factor in the moral life of the contemporary Christian.

Fourth, *agape* remains always the fundamental attitude of the Christian. Perhaps too often today one speaks of the law of love and the law of the Spirit without realizing the concrete demands of love in a given situation. *Agape* includes the willingness to give oneself for others. The attitude of the Christian towards the laws of the Christian community must be a meditation of love. Christian love demands the willingness to make personal sacrifices for the good of others. Christians must even see the inherent imperfections in Church law as an opportunity to live the Paschal Mystery in the dying to self in the service of others. *Epikeia* in the context of *agape* can never lead to selfishness and egoistic individualism.

What about abuses? There will be abuses, even glaring abuses. However, the old theological axiom remains true: *abusus non tollit usum. Epikeia* is the great virtue of Christian freedom and Christian responsibility. The Christian must stand on his own two feet and make the decisions himself with regard to the obligations of Church laws in particular circumstances. Naturally, he will be guided by the counsel and actions of others in the Christian community. However, the ultimate decision rests with the individual. The freedom and responsibility entailed in the proper understanding of *epikeia* is the same freedom and responsibility which the free call of God in Christ presupposes. God could have corralled all men into salvation, but he chose to freely call man to a life of community with himself and all mankind. The divine plan of salvation has tried to safeguard personal responsibility and freedom. Sin is the terrible abuse of man's freedom, and yet God was willing to accept the horrible consequences of sin rather than do away with man's responsibility. The abuses connected with *epikeia* can never constitute a sufficient reason to deny the need for *epikeia* in the life of the Christian.

Why all the stress on *epikeia* today? There are many reasons contributing to the greater need for the virtue of *epikeia* today. As already mentioned, the tensions between the individual and the community are much greater today than in the past. Likewise, theology now realizes the ancillary role of law in the Church, but much of the present legislation reflects a mentality that practically equates life in the Christian community with the observance of positive law. Also, the stress on individual responsibility is being recognized in all of theology. When people were truly the unlettered masses, they were not able to make their own decisions. Just a few centuries ago, all life was structured from the top down. The individual person who lacked adequate knowledge and education always looked to the authorities to find out what he should do. In such circumstances, the greatest stress was put on dispensations, privileges, and recourse to the will of the legislator. Today, privileges and dispensations have no real meaning when they concern laws that affect only individuals. In fact, some of the privileges connected with certain organizations are a source of scandal, especially today. If membership in a certain society gives me the privilege of not praying the breviary under certain conditions, there is no reason why as a mature Christian I cannot make the judgment that in particular situations I am not bound to the canonical law of praying the breviary.

The complexity and responsibility which characterize modern life require that the individual Christian make the final decision in a particular situation involving a positive law of the Church. The individual Catholic must respect and follow the laws of the Church, but a true understanding recognizes the provisional and imperfect nature of Church law. The virtue of *epikeia* moderates the literalness and inapplicability of the law in the face of the very real Christian demands in a concrete situation. *Epikeia* is a virtue of Christian maturity and responsibility. A true understanding of *epikeia* should avoid false extremes of legalism and anarchy. *Epikeia* is the practical functioning of the law of the Spirit, the primary law of the Christian life, in the context of the positive law of the Church.

The Moral Theology
of Bernard Häring

Chapter Five

Bernard Häring is the one name most frequently associated with the renewal of moral theology. Häring played an influential role in the work of Vatican II, and in many ways the German Redemptorist theologian epitomizes the Council with its many accomplishments and its shortcomings. The Ecumenical Council was primarily pastoral in tone and scope—trying to make the Church more relevant in the contemporary world. Häring too is primarily pastoral in his approach to moral theology.

The Vatican Council's most lasting contribution will probably be in the attitudes and orientations it has encouraged. The Fathers of the Council constantly stressed the pastoral and not the dogmatic purpose of the Council. Häring has not really evolved any new moral theories or systems of ethical thinking. Rather, he is the embodiment of openness and dialogue with the contemporary society which so characterized the Council. Future theologians will probably cite

Häring's specific teachings rather infrequently. Häring, like the Council, represents a beginning and not an end. *The Law of Christ*, his three volume *magnum opus* of moral theology, is definitely transitional in character.

Above all, Häring has given a new orientation to moral theology. Moral theology as taught in Catholic seminaries (and reductively on all educational levels) until the last decade had the rather limited scope of training future confessors as judges in the confessional. The predecessors of the seminary manuals of theology were the *Institutiones Theologiae Moralis*, which came into existence at the end of the sixteenth century. The original *Institutiones Theologiae Moralis* were in themselves an *aggiornamento*—a creative response to the needs of the time. The Council of Trent, which tried to renew the meaning and practice of the sacrament of penance, decreed that all Catholics must receive the sacrament of penance once a year. Penance required the confession of all mortal sins according to their number and species. (One must admit that the teaching of Trent on penance is rather one-sided and overly juridical.)

The Society of Jesus (Jesuits) was instrumental in putting into practice the reforms of Trent. The Jesuits introduced a curriculum of studies which called for a two year course in practical moral theology to train confessors especially for their role as judges in the sacrament of penance. The classes taught by the Jesuit professors evolved into the *Institutiones Theologiae Moralis*. These manuals emphasized what constituted sin and the differences between mortal and venial sins. Their tone and outlook was negative, minimalistic, and legalistic. Perhaps the main problem was that subsequent generations of theologians accepted these manuals as the totality of moral theology despite their very limited scope and purpose.

In the nineteenth century a reaction set in against the negative attitude, the legalistic approach, and the overly casuistic methodology of the manuals of moral theology. The first attempts at renewal began in Germany with the works of John Michael Sailer (1751-1832) and John Baptist Hirscher (1788-1865). The Tübingen school in Germany continued to develop the thought of the two pioneers. However, the work of the Tübingen school was almost unknown outside Germany; and even in Germany itself the older manuals of theology were standard fare in many seminaries. The twentieth century brought more attempts, both inside and outside Germany, to renew moral theology. However, Bernard Häring is the theologian who eventually made Catholic thinking aware of the renewal of moral theology. *The Law of Christ*, Häring's systematic treatment of moral theology, first appeared in Germany in 1954. The original German has gone through seven editions and has been translated into at least eight other languages.

Many factors have contributed to Häring's prominence in the field of moral theology at the present time. Häring impresses all who meet him as a dedicated Christian with a sensitive love for his fellow man. The German Redemptorist earned his own degree in theology at the University of Tübingen in 1947, where he came into contact with the pioneering efforts to renew moral theology. Perhaps even more significant were his earlier experiences. Häring, who was born in Bötingen in 1912, was ordained a Redemptorist priest in the late 1930's. However, during the war he served as a medic in the German army and also ministered to the spiritual needs of the soldiers. After the war he worked with displaced persons in Poland. A man with such a background could never be content with a moral theology which was enunciated in the isolation of religious houses and seemed to have no contact with the daily life of humanity. Since 1950, Häring has published articles and books amounting to an average of more than 300 pages per year. He has lectured extensively throughout Europe and both Americas.

Häring could devote all his time to academic scholarship, but his primarily pastoral orientation shows through in the countless conferences, institutes and retreats he has given all over the globe. Some of Häring's writings seem superficial and betray a rather hasty preparation. Häring would probably defend such books and articles, despite their obvious shortcomings, as another way of bringing the renewal in Catholic life and thinking to an ever wider audience.

The central idea in Häring's moral theology is response and responsibility. The Christian life is man's response to the gift of God in Christ. The dialogical character of the Christian life reflects the covenant between God and his people—man faithfully responds to the divine initiative.

God's loving call is primary in Häring's ethical thought. The life of the Christian is not merely a eudaemonistic self-fulfillment nor the dutiful performance of divine obligations. By emphasizing the primacy of God's love, Häring avoids the danger of pelagianism which lurks in some of the manuals of moral theology. Man does not save himself by his own works and efforts; rather, he is saved by the merciful love of the Father through the redemptive activity of Christ. The moral life is man's response to the new life received in Christ Jesus. Man the responder must always remain open to receive the continual gift of God's love. Poverty of spirit, humility of heart, marks the fundamental disposition of the Christian. The follower of Christ is ever vigilant and open to the call of God in his daily life.

Worship and thanksgiving characterize the Christian life precisely because of the divine initiative in salvation. Häring's writings constantly emphasize the connection between liturgy and life. In the liturgy man comes into contact with the new life of the Risen Christ. Liturgy as the reenactment of the Christian mystery underlines the primacy of the divine initiative in salvation. The frequently misunderstood axiom of sacramental theology—*ex opere operato*—illustrates the primary truth that salvation is a work worked by God. Liturgy, especially the sacramental encounter, exemplifies in itself the dialogical character of the Christian life. The word and work of God call man to respond in his own word and work. The sacraments are efficacious signs of God's love, the visibility of grace. Since God obliges man by the gifts he gives, the sacramental sign points out the nature of the gift and the nature of the response. Liturgy and life reinforce one another. Man's participation and response in the liturgy become meaningless unless accompanied by a response to God's call in daily living. Likewise, the Christian life is a life of worship, a life which recognizes that all the things of this world are God's gift to man. Man realizing the divine bounty praises God by his use of the goods of this world in the service of the kingdom.

Conversion (*metanoia*), the change of heart, represents the Christian's response to the loving call of God. The primary function of the Church is to preach the good news of conversion. Too often in the past a moralizing preaching and a legalistic approach have characterized the proclamation of the Christian message. The Church in her liturgy, life, and witness must proclaim the gospel—the good news of salvation.

Häring boldly teaches that the universal vocation of all Christians to perfection is the fundamental consideration in moral theology. Conversion is not just a once for all time action, but rather a continual conversion is the law of life for the Christian. The Christian constantly seeks to share more fully in the Paschal Mystery and in the love of God and neighbor. Häring vigorously attacks the theory that only a few Christians are called to perfection. All those called to perfection do not leave the world and live in monasteries to follow the evangelical counsels while the majority of ordinary Christians are content to remain in the world and merely obey the ten commandments.

Since all Christians are called to perfection, Häring realizes the importance of the so called everyday life of the ordinary man in the world. Daily existence and the world in which we live are related to the kingdom of God. Man is called in his daily life to make the kingdom more and more present. The world is not just a stage on which man works out the eternal salvation of his soul. The whole world belongs to the creative and redemptive work of God. The Christian is called to continue the creative and reconciling action of the Lord of history. Work, culture, art, science, politics, and all truly human activities have a meaning and an importance for the kingdom and the Christian, since the Christian is called to build up now the new heaven and the new earth. Redemption is cosmic and social as well as individual.

Häring's consideration of the social order illustrates the social and cosmic dimensions of the Christian life. All the goods of creation are inherently social and communal, since they exist fundamentally for the good of all mankind. No social system is just if it deprives men or groups of men of those earthly goods which are necessary for a truly human existence. In this light, Häring considers the defects of both socialism and liberalistic capitalism. Although admitting the right to private property, provided it is limited by the social aspect of all earthly goods, Häring flatly states that in the light of the Christian ideal the present order of property is in need of radical change. The rich nations of the world are reminded of their obligations to the developing countries. Socialization and land reform are also necessary to bring about a more equitable distribution of the goods of this world.

The communitarian aspect of the Christian life assumes an important place in Häring's theology. Salvation comes to man in community, as a member of the Church, the new Israel. The love which characterizes Christian life is above all seen in community, the willingness to share what we have with others. The beneficiaries of the divine *agape* must be willing to share what they have with others. The communitarian aspect of the Christian life also underlines the social aspects of Christian existence in the present world.

Growth and dynamism, not mere conformity, mark the life of the Christian. No true follower of Christ can ever say that he has observed the law of Christ perfectly from his youth. The law of Christ demands a continual conversion and development. Häring consequently rejects a morality based *entirely* on universal norms applicable to all men. Häring accepts and vigorously defends the universal, negative prohibitions that have been traditionally taught in Catholic moral theology; but these norms merely mark out the outside limits of the Christian life. They show the few actions which will always be incompatible with the new life received in Christ Jesus. Within these boundaries the individual Christian is called to respond according to the individual talents and gifts he has received.

Häring develops a situation ethics based on the *kairos*, which, however, does not deny the existence of the traditional absolutes in the Christian life. The *kairos* is the unique call of God to the individual Christian in his particular situation. The *kairos* corresponds to the individual elements in the situation, the particular gifts given by God to the individual. The individual and unique call of the *kairos*, however, does not contradict the generic obligations based on the humanity which all men share in common.

The German Redemptorist acknowledges the overemphasis on the particular, external act in the manuals of moral theology. The particular human act achieves the fullness of meaning insofar as it is revelatory of the human person. Man is a composite being, an embodied spirit. Man communicates and expresses himself in and through his corporality. True moral value arises from the depths of the human person, but an ethic of pure inwardness which pays attention only to the motive and intention of the person is false. Man's external actions make his heart visible. But man also bears a responsibility to the order of the world to which he contributes by his external actions. A species of legalism insists only on the external action in itself apart from the person. A false quietism and underevaluation of worldly existence ignore the value of the external action as such. Häring maintains that only values related to the person are moral in the strict sense, but objective values are also morally meaningful as bearers of moral values.

Häring applies the same understanding of the values involved in human acts to the question of sin. Too often in the past Catholic theologians identified sin with a particular, external action. It is a sin to lie, to steal, to fornicate. Häring does not deny that such actions are wrong, but sin is not primarily a thing or an external action. Scripture and theology indicate that sin involves a deeply personal reality, the breaking of man's relationship with God. Just as *metanoia* or conversion involves a change of heart by which man turns to God, so sin involves a change of heart in breaking the relationship of love with God. The external action makes visible the reality of the change of heart. Catholic theology has admitted a distinction between mortal and venial sin. Mortal sin breaks man's relationship with God and ultimately leads to total death and separation from God. The older emphasis in distinguishing mortal sin from venial sin fell on the gravity of the matter involved. If the action is grave matter (theft, adultery), the sin is grave. If the action is light matter (lying, slight disrespect), the sin is venial. Häring, however, argues that the ultimate distinction between mortal and venial sin lies in the subjective involvement of the person. Mortal sin engages the core of the person, the fundamental project of his existence; whereas venial sin remains a somewhat peripheral action which does not totally involve the person as such.

There has always been in Catholic thought an ambivalence about the word sin. Sometimes sin refers to the breaking of the person's relationship of love with God; whereas at other times sin refers to external actions which are wrong. Häring's theory opts for the first approach, although he also uses sin just to describe a wrong action considered in itself apart from the subject. Perhaps Häring could have taken a more definitive forward step by consistently reserving sin to the breaking of man's relationship with God.

Catholic moral theology has often been branded as legalistic. The theology manuals frequently give credence to that charge. Häring provoked much controversy among some Catholic theologians by his treatment of Church law although in reality his teaching on Church law follows the scholastic understanding of the nature of human law. St. Thomas taught that every human law admits of exceptions precisely because of the contingent circumstances which might enter into a particular situation. Häring merely re-echoes the whole Christian tradition in affirming the primacy of the internal law of the Holy Spirit dwelling in the hearts of the just and the secondary and relative character of any human law. Human Church law is never obliging if it stands in the way of the primary law of *agape*. Catholic life and theology in the past have come to grips with the need for exceptions to human law by an emphasis on dispensations, privileges, and excusing factors. Häring and other contemporary theologians stress the role of the virtue of *epikeia* in conflict situations in which the letter of the human law seems to impede the true spirit of the law. *Epikeia* places the ultimate responsibility on the individual person himself to decide if the letter of the law is obliging in a particular situation.

What about Häring's position on the natural law? In general, Häring accepts the traditional Catholic understanding of the natural law, but he incorporates the natural law into his more biblically inspired, dialogical understanding of the Christian life. The natural gifts of creation which man has received from God call for a fitting response. Man acts in accord with the nature that he has received from God. The existence of some negative, absolute norms of conduct does not necessarily imply a legalism or code morality. Such negative norms merely point out the few actions which are never compatible with our human existence. Within the large field of human actions which are compatible with our human nature, there are no general principles from which man can always deduce what is the fitting thing to do. Under the inspiration of the Spirit man is led to embrace those actions which are most fitting in the particular situation.

Häring does incorporate most of the contemporary Catholic insights on natural law theory and thus avoids the stereotyped versions of natural law that frequently appear in textbooks. The natural law does not necessarily preclude any growth or development. Historicity and evolution also characterize human nature. Häring is also careful to show that natural law is not identified with biological processes. For example, he objects to the heretofore almost unanimous opinion of Catholic theologians that masturbation for seminal analysis is wrong.

Häring staunchly defends the absolute moral norms that have been taught by Catholic theologians—sterilization, direct abortion, divorce, etc. Occasionally in such problems, e.g., sterilization, he admits that for a particular individual there might be no sin because of the subjective circumstances involved. The distinction between objective and subjective guilt has been traditionally maintained in Catholic theology. Even though an action is wrong, for a particular person here and now it might not be sinful. Häring also justifies such a distinction by his theory of growth. Particular circumstances might prevent a person from doing the fullness of what is required at the present time. If he cannot do everything the norm demands, he should do whatever is possible and hold himself open for future growth so that he can then fulfill the demands of the law. Occasionally one wonders if Häring does not employ the distinction between objective and subjective sin as a means of avoiding the difficult moral problem of the existence of such absolute norms as sterilization.

Häring generally accepts the traditional natural law solutions to moral problems—the application of the principle of direct and indirect effects to the question of killing; the just war theory; euthanasia. In his understanding of truth telling and lying, Häring rejects the theory of *falsioquium* that would define lying in terms of the neighbor's right to truth. He maintains that any false utterance is a lie. Although Häring tries to argue from the divine source of truth, the value of personal uprightness, and the need for trustworthiness in the community, one wonders if he is not influenced mostly by the seemingly faulty "faculty argument" which finds the malice of lying in the misuse of the faculty of speech.

Any critique of *The Law of Christ* must take into consideration the fact that the work first appeared almost fifteen years ago. The last fifteen years have witnessed a tremendous change in Catholic theology. To Häring's credit, he called for many of these changes long before they became the popular slogans of the era of Vatican II. However, *The Law of*

Christ betrays its age and reveals its transitional character. Häring has taken the traditional moral theology with its strongly scholastic, philosophical underpinnings and put it in the larger context of a scripturally based, covenant relationship between God and man. Häring also adds occasional insights from personalist and existentialist philosophy. An interest in religious sociology helps Häring to make moral theology more relevant to the problems of contemporary society. Häring's broader scope also encourages him to treat some matters pertaining to human life which were ordinarily not mentioned in the manuals of moral theology which were interested almost exclusively in training confessors.

The Law of Christ begins with a study of theological anthropology and then discusses freedom as the basis of the human response. Häring, following the general pattern of moral theology textbooks, then considers conscience, the human action, law, the moral object, and sin. The first volume ends with a discussion of the virtues which is a good example in miniature of Häring's approach. He follows the traditional division of the cardinal virtues, but he never loses the Christian perspective in this discussion. However, to the four cardinal virtues Häring adds a section on humility as the basic Christian attitude of those who have received life and salvation as a gift of God. The first volume in English corresponds to what is generally called general moral theology, which treats the orientation and basis of moral theology.

The second and third volumes comprise the area of special moral theology, which investigates the particular aspects and actions of the Christian life. The English translation divides the life of the Christian under the two headings of "Life in Fellowship with God," which embraces man's relationship with God and roughly coincides with the first three commandments, and "Love in Human Fellowship," which considers man in his relationship with his neighbor and the world, and very roughly corresponds to the matter of the second table of the decalogue.

It is always difficult to assess the influence and real significance of any contemporary. The task is even more difficult in the present case since the appraiser has been privileged to have Father Bernard Häring as his professor and mentor. I do not believe that future theologians will frequently refer to Häring's moral system or even to his theological analysis of particular attitudes and actions in the Christian life. Perhaps this is the fate of all those who are constantly considering the problems of the present day in the light of the Christian message. However, Häring, more than anyone else, has helped to change the attitude and orientation of moral theology. Like Vatican II, Häring is primarily pastoral; and like the Vatican Council, Häring marks a beginning rather than an end.

Dialogue with
Joseph Fletcher

Chapter Six

This chapter makes no pretensions about solving the problems of situation ethics. The scope is much narrower. First, it will attempt to situate the problem of situation ethics. Having delineated the problem, a dialogue will ensue. The dialogue will first investigate the rigidity attached to natural law in the tradition of Catholic moral theology and then will question some of the presuppositions of Joseph Fletcher's situation ethics. Finally, some tentative conclusions for moral theology will be drawn.

SITUATING THE PROBLEM

What is the precise area of practical disagreement between the proponents of situation ethics and traditional Catholic moral theology? Disagreement centers on the existence of negative, universal prohibitions concerning ethical conduct. Catholic theology has traditionally upheld such norms

whereas situation ethicians claim that love is the only absolute. The exact areas of disagreement would include human
sexuality, prohibitions based on the distinction of direct and
indirect, questions concerning the taking of human life, and
divorce.

However, there are vast areas of practical agreement. Catholic theology realizes that the majority of man's moral decisions are not based on the application of determined, universal norms to particular cases. Catholic theologians teach
that the negative, universal norms merely serve as the boundary lines within which the ethical life of the Christian must
be lived. Certain actions are not in keeping with the new
life received in Christ Jesus. Just as there are certain actions
that a mother would never perform, so too there are certain
actions which a Christian should never do. Within these extreme limits, all ethical decisions are arrived at in a situa-
tionalist manner.

In the past Catholic life has often suffered from legalism.
The Catholic was the one who obeyed the laws of God and
the Church. However, today all realize the horrible carica-
ture in reducing the Christian life to the observance of a
few negative commandments. Catholic theology, however,
has always taught that a human law, by its very nature, admits of exceptions. Since human laws are based on what
generally happens for most people, they must admit of exceptions. Even concerning the natural law, most moral decisions are not based on universal norms, for the norms are
generally negative and merely tell us some few things that
we must always avoid. The universal laws cannot positively
tell us the exact and fitting decision to make in the particular situation. The number of such negative, universal norms
is quite few. Even the prohibitions against killing and abortion have been limited to direct abortion and direct killing.

The dialogue over situationalism must avoid caricatures and false arguments. For example, some situationists show the absurdity of an absolute norm against lying.[1] In certain situations it seems that man must tell a lie; for example, the captured soldier who is asked about vital information. However, the defenders of an absolute prohibition against lying can come to the same conclusions as situationists. It all depends how one defines a lie! If the malice of lying consists in the violation of my neighbor's right to truth and not in the conformity of the spoken word with my thought, then "principlists" and situationalists can agree on the question of truth telling in particular situations.[2]

Frequently, the opponents of the new morality will accuse the situationists of anarchy and antinomianism. Such charges can be most misleading. The situationist is a responsible person who is honestly striving to respond in a Christian manner. Situationists do not believe that man can do whatever his whim and fancy might wish. Christians are always obliged to do the most loving thing in the particular situation.

Occasionally, situationists propose the problem in terms of love versus law. Joseph Fletcher inaccurately states the problem in terms of the opposing methodologies of legalism and situationalism.[3] Such a formulation of the problem is totally unfair. The "principlist" would never admit that the law or principle should always be followed even when love would demand something else. The question is not one of law versus love. Rather the proper question is: does love demand constant, uniform ways of acting? Are there certain actions which are always incompatible with love? Most situationists would admit some general ways of acting that are always incompatible with love; e.g., real disrespect for neighbor. The problem centers on the very few, specific, universal prohibitions. Likewise, the two positions cannot be characterized as code morality versus wisdom morality. To admit that certain actions are incompatible with Christian existence does not mean that one subscribes to code morality. Charges and countercharges of antinomianism and legalism do not help to clarify the rather limited but none the less real differences between situation ethics and traditional Catholic moral theology.

CRITIQUE OF NATURAL LAW

Having situated the problem of situation ethics, we will now investigate the purported source of the insistence on absolute norms in Catholic moral theology. Both Catholics and non-Catholics claim that the natural law is responsible for the insistence on absolute norms in Catholic theology.[4] However, a historical consideration will reveal that natural law as such does not adequately explain the emphasis on absolute norms in Catholic theology. Note well that I am not saying that absolute norms are wrong, but I merely contend that natural law as such cannot adequately explain and justify such norms. The following few paragraphs will summarize, in a somewhat different manner, the understanding of natural law developed at greater length in Chapter Three.

Too often Catholic theologians talk as if the natural law were a monolithic philosophical system with an agreed upon body of ethical content spelled out in minute detail. It is true that philosophers from Aristotle to the present day have employed the term natural law, but the theory itself has had many different meanings in the course of history. One Catholic commentator lists twenty different senses in which the word natural has been used even by Catholics![5] When Paul in the letter to the Romans says that the Gentiles do by nature what was commanded by the law, the Apostle to the Gentiles does not give a stamp of approval to the theory proposed by St. Thomas thirteen centuries later. Paul merely uses the term in a very popular and unphilosophical way.

Aristotle believed in a rational order, but he placed the reason of the order in the specific nature of the individual. The Stoics also had a natural law teaching, but their order existed primarily in the cosmos, the whole universe. The definition attributed to Ulpian, the great Roman lawyer, understands natural law as that which is common to man and all the animals. Ulpian's definition is definitely open to the charge of biologism and the canonization of animal processes. Gratian, the monk who codified the laws of the Church in the twelfth century, claims that the natural law is the golden rule as it is found in the law and the gospel. Even after St. Thomas, both inside and outside Catholic circles, different meanings were attached to the term natural law. Catholics must admit that least for the greater part of the Church's existence, there was not a coherent philosophical system called the natural law. I do not deny that the term natural law does indicate some basic human tendencies and attitudes that have been present in the history of man, but such attitudes are not very sharply defined.

Even the Thomistic understanding of natural law is much less absolute than the versions of natural law in Catholic theology manuals. Thomas admits as a matter of principle that once reason leaves first principles and descends to particulars, there is a possibility of defects occurring.[6] Jacques Maritain reacts against the notion that the natural law is a moral code.[7] Another Thomist, Columba Ryan, O.P., argues that "the derivative principles of the natural law are either so general as to provide little guidance to conduct or else so disputable as to win no general consent. . . ."[8]

Perhaps the greatest fallacy is that the Catholic Church has used the theory of natural law as the vehicle or instrument of arriving at its moral teachings. A simple historical reflection recalls that the vast majority of the moral teachings of the Church were formulated long before Thomas enunciated his theory of natural law! The teaching on divorce, fornication, killing etc. was not hammered out in a meeting or seminar of natural law theoreticians called together to investigate a particular moral problem. For the most part the individual teachings existed long before the Thomistic understanding of natural law. Theologians later used the concept of natural law to bolster the teachings which had originally been arrived at independently of natural law. Only since the last century has natural law been regularly invoked by the magisterium as the vehicle by which the hierarchical magisterium reasons to its moral teaching.[9] These papal teachings have generally centered on the two areas of medical-moral problems and social ethics. Today Catholic theologians are questioning many of the present teachings in the area of medical morals. The very restrained use of the term natural law in the Pastoral Constitution on the Church in the Modern World indicates that the Fathers of the Vatican Council do not claim to have derived their social teachings from the application of a strict natural law theory.[10]

Most of the present moral teaching of the Catholic Church, including the absolute norms, did not come into existence through an application of natural law theory to particular moral problems. Catholic theologians then cannot adequately explain such absolutes by appeal to the natural law theory. Likewise, just because one such absolute is eliminated, it does not follow that the other absolutes are also unwarranted. Each of the few absolutes in Catholic moral teaching must be examined in itself; any generic appeal to natural law seems unwarranted. The natural law as such cannot adequately explain the existence of absolute norms and the insistence on such norms in moral theology.

The question of particular absolute norms will be discussed at greater length in the epilogue. Problems seem to arise in the area of negative, moral absolutes; that is, forbidden actions which are defined in non-moral terms and sometimes defined merely in terms of the physical or biological structure of the act itself. The epilogue calls into question some aspects of the present Catholic teaching on divorce, medical ethics, and conflict situations involving killing or abortion which are decided by an application of the principle of the indirect voluntary. In these cases I can agree with some of the strictures made by Fletcher and other situationalists.

CRITIQUE OF PROFESSOR FLETCHER

Now to direct the dialogue to Professor Fletcher. I will consider three difficulties I find in the ethical presuppositions enunciated by Fletcher; the notion of love or *agape*, extrinsicism or nominalism, and pragmatism.

According to Fletcher *agape* or loving concern is the only norm for the Christian. *Agape* describes the complete willingness to give oneself to others the same way that Christ has given himself for us. *Agape* is distinguished from romantic love (*eros*) and friendship love (*philia*) precisely because *agape* is incompatible with any aspiring or self-seeking love. Reciprocity, mutuality and friendship do not enter into the notion of *agape*. Fletcher seems to draw too exalted a picture of *agape*.[11] He definitely does not solve the age-old problem of the relationship between *agape* and proper love of self. His description of *agape* appears to be even a-human and would always demand the heroic on the part of man.

Paradoxically, the exalted notion of *agape* does not seem to enter into the final decisions made by the Christian situationist. Is *agape* really as important as Fletcher says? One could start with a very human idea of wisdom or justice and come to the same practical conclusions as Fletcher. *Agape* in theory appears to transcend all human wisdom and human values, but in practice *agape* does not really differ that much from human wisdom.

From a methodological viewpoint, Fletcher makes the revealed notion of *agape* the sole guiding element in Christian morality. But is there not a huge area of common ground morality which Christians share with all men of good will? Christianity and secular humanism can agree on many points, but Fletcher's system allows no room for the dialogue with humanism. *Agape* is the distinctive note in Christian ethics, but the insistence on *agape* as the only way into the ethical problem eliminates the whole scope of human wisdom existing apart from explicit revelation of the scriptures.

Secondly, an extrinsic or nominalistic approach to ethics. Fletcher denies that there are any values at all. There are only things which happen to be valued by persons.[12] Extrinsicism maintains that all meaning and value come from outside the thing itself. I maintain that earthly realities do have a value and meaning in themselves apart from the meaning given them by the intention of a particular person. The whole theory of incarnational spirituality reminds us of the importance of the things of this world. Earthly realities do have a meaning. Here and now the Christian is called upon to build up the new heaven and the new earth. The world is not just a stage full of props on which men work out their eternal destinies. Rather, earthly values have a part to play in the shaping of the new heaven and the new earth. I do not think that Fletcher takes earthly reality seriously enough. To phrase the same objection in another way: you cannot have Teilhard and Fletcher too!

Not only a Teilhardian view of the world but also common sense tells us that things have a value in themselves apart from the intention of the person. How often do we say that a big heart does not excuse stupidity. Everyone of us has suffered from well intentioned people who have done the wrong thing. We are constantly reminded that intention is not enough. Things do have some meaning in themselves, and what we do is important. A highly technological age realizes that intentions can never justify the lack of competency. The moral problem of poverty in the world and poverty in America will never be solved by good intentions. There are some ways of trying to solve the problem that are better than others. Man must creatively employ the proper means to bring about his desired intentions and goals.

In the past I will admit that Catholic theology has sometimes acted as if all the meaning and value were intrinsic in things themselves. This has led to the occasional canonization of physical acts and processes. This danger of naturalism seems present in some of the arguments advanced against artificial contraception. Likewise, the opinion that masturbation for seminal analysis is wrong seems to canonize a natural process. However, the problem is not solved by going to the opposite extreme and saying there is no meaning or value in reality apart from the intention of the persons involved. It seems to me there has to be a mutual interplay between the person and the reality which he is confronting. Perhaps here again Catholic theology has over exaggerated the meaning of intrinsic morality. Intrinsic morality does not mean the object in the abstract is always right or wrong. Rather, the whole moral complex, the situation, if you will, is right or wrong apart from the intention of the person. Perhaps there is not as much disagreement with Fletcher on this point as there might seem to be at first sight.

Thirdly, pragmatism. Pragmatism is the first of the four presuppositions mentioned by Fletcher. "Pragmatism is, to be plain spoken, a *practical* or *success* posture. Its idiom expresses the genius and ethos or style of life of American culture and of the techno-scientific era."[13] Fletcher tries to wed pragmatism and *agape*, but I do not think they are totally compatible. Pragmatism is success oriented in the sense of producing successful results as quickly as possible. Pragmatism will do anything to achieve its purpose. For example, in warfare, sheer pragmatism will say that you should end the war as quickly and effectively as possible. If this involves killing innocent people in a wholesale manner, such killing will have to be done. In a pragmatically oriented society, what happens to those who through handicap or old age are no longer able to contribute to the success of the society? Can such people be dispensed with as a drag and burden on the society which is striving to be successful?

Fletcher may rightly claim that pragmatism is only a method and says nothing about content. However, Fletcher is loathe to speak about the content of love. To be pragmatically Christian means to bring about the success of true *agape*, but the Christian notion of success lies in the shadow of the cross of Christ. The Paschal Mystery is the success story for the Christian, but such a life requires a dying to self. Is there enough room for the cross and suffering in the system proposed by Fletcher? Even the theological advocates of the secular city realize the need for the transcendent judgment of Christianity. The secular city with all its pragmatism can set up its own false idols which have to be criticized in the light of the Christian message.[14] I do not think that Christianity and a totally pragmatic outlook without an accurate delineation of the content of *agape* are entirely compatible. If by pragmatic, one means only that the Christian must find the most creative ways of showing *agape* in the modern world, I agree. But Fletcher is unable to tell us the exact meaning and content of *agape*.

A THEOLOGY OF COMPROMISE

What can moral theology learn from a dialogue with Joseph Fletcher? At the very least situation ethics has been a good corrective for traditional moral theology. The average Christian makes almost all his ethical decisions within the boundary lines of the Christian life marked off by the few negative, universal prohibitions. Creativity and not conformity must be more present in the lives of most of us Christians. Situation ethics is a constant reminder to avoid the pitfalls of a shallow legalism.

Joseph Fletcher's approach does reflect a way of looking at reality which is more suitable to modern man than the approach frequently employed in moral theology. The classical philosophy underlying much of moral theology tends to emphasize the permanent, the essential, the unchanging, and the substantial. Modern man places more emphasis on the historical, the particular, the individual, the changing, and the relational. The classical approach is primarily deductive; whereas modern man tends to be inductive. The inductive approach is more probing and less dogmatic than the deductive. I do not conclude that there are no absolute, negative norms of ethical conduct; but the modern way of looking at reality is less favorable to such norms than the older, classical world view.

In the past few years Catholic moralists have been more conscious of the strains created by some absolute affirmations in Catholic theology. Catholic theologians admit the danger of identifying the human act with mere biological processes. Perhaps Catholic theology has exaggerated the old axiom that the end does not justify the means. There are cases in which the end specifies the means just as there are cases in which the end does not justify the means. The theory of the indirect voluntary, the difference between direct and indirect effects, has been called into question and examination.[15] Theologians are asking for a reconsideration of the teaching of the Catholic Church on divorce. Archbishop Denis Hurley has recently proposed the theory of the overriding right to solve the conflicts and dilemmas which so often arise because of conflicting rights.[16] These questions are developed at greater length elsewhere in this book. Now I want to develop a theory of compromise morality.

In general, I think that within the continuity of traditional moral theology I can substantially agree with many, although not all—especially in the area of human sexuality—of the practical solutions mentioned by Professor Fletcher in his writings. However, I have definite reservations about some aspects of his methodology as mentioned above; and I feel uneasy at the general tone created in his attitude of exceptions to general rules. Fletcher makes the exception the rule! Perhaps such an attitude comes from the obviously polemical nature of his controversy with his opponents. In reacting to them, he seems to overreact.

How is it possible to find substantial agreement from within the Catholic tradition with many of the conclusions reached by Professor Fletcher? Catholic theology has admitted a distinction between formal sin and material sin. Material sins are actions which are wrong, but because of mitigating circumstances are not imputable to the person. Such actions are objectively wrong, but not subjectively sinful. On a popular level the existence of that distinction is shown in the remark that there is all the difference in the world between what the priest says in the pulpit and what he says in the confessional. Certainly no confessor would act harshly toward the woman who bore an illegitimate child to free herself from the concentration camp and the danger of death.

Catholic moral theology also acknowledges the possibility of choosing the lesser of two evils where there are no other viable alternatives in a conflict situation. Therefore, the actions which Fletcher would call good, Catholic theology would say are objectively wrong, but not subjectively sinful, or they are the lesser of two evils. But I think that Catholic theology might even go further. How?

Catholic moral theology claims to be a realistic ethic. (I believe one can still maintain such an ethic and not fall into the "is-ought" problem raised by Hume.) Theology today, however, is much more conscious of the presence and reality of sin in the world.[17] Sin incarnates itself in the structures of human society. Sin contaminates the very air we breathe. The sin of the world must be a factor in any realistic approach to Christian ethics. As an example, when the majority of students are cheating on an examination, the individual in a sense has to cheat or else put himself at an unfair position vis-a-vis the others.

Historically, traditional theology has had a difficult time coming to grips with the moral dilemmas where sin and evil were obviously very present. In fact, one of the major impetuses to situation ethics has come from the inability of traditional Christian ethics to deal with such sin-filled situations. Experience in the underground, in concentration camps, in resistance movements, and in war have made some Christians think at times theft, forgery, adultery, abortion, and killing were good actions which were humanly necessary in such situations.

How can moral theology come to grips with ethical decisions in such sin-filled situations? I believe that a theory of compromise is in continuity with the tradition of Catholic theology. In the face of the sinful situation man must do the best he can. The destructive and disruptive influence of sin frequently prevents man from doing what he would want to do in the given situation. The business man might be forced to make kickbacks in order to stay in business. The laborer might have to kick in so much a day to be hired. The word compromise seems to fit such situations quite well. From one viewpoint the act is good because it is the best that one can do. However, from the other aspect the act is wrong and shows the presence of sin in the given situation which the Christian is continually called upon to overcome.

Fletcher will object that a compromise theory is typical of of an intrinsic approach to morality. I agree. However, his own approach seems to dismiss too easily the sinfulness and the wrong present in the situation. When a woman is forced to have an abortion to save her life there is something wrong in that situation. When one must kill to protect innocent victims of mass hatred, there is something sinful and wrong about the situation. When a woman in Harlem is deprived of every source of human happiness except having a child out of wedlock, there is something wrong with the situation. Those sinful situations must be overcome. Fletcher dismisses the whole problem too easily by saying that the particular action is not wrong. Under one aspect, the action is not wrong; but under another aspect the action is wrong and manifests the sinfulness of the situation.

The theory of compromise tries to do justice to the total situation, especially to the social aspects of the situation. Fletcher's approach is too individualistic and does not take sufficient cognizance of the social aspect of man's life in the world. Society and the individual's milieu influence his decision and are affected by his personal decisions. Man has a responsibility for the society in which he lives. As a general critique, perhaps one could say that Fletcher does not give sufficient attention to the social aspects of man's moral life. Note the absence of references to questions of peace, urban poverty, the rights of minorities, discriminatory practices in housing and employment, and guaranteed annual wage, to mention but a few. Ethicians who have been more concerned with social questions (e.g., Reinhold Niebuhr and John C. Bennett) have been more ready to admit some principles other than love and have not defended such an extrinsic understanding of morality.

Compromise also indicates that the person cannot be entirely at ease in making such a decision. In a sense the Christian always has an uneasy conscience. Every such decision indicates that sin is somehow forcing a person to do what he would prefer not to do under other circumstances. Compromise adopts a middle course between the teaching of the manuals of moral theology and the theory of Professor Fletcher. The moral theology manuals would maintain that such an action is always wrong. Fletcher would maintain that the action is good. Compromise maintains that in a sense the action is good because the person can do nothing else at the present time. However, in a certain sense the action is wrong and manifests the presence of sin in the world.

In a theory of compromise the Christian must take the risk of responsible decision making. Is the existing sinful structure such that I must compromise or am I merely deceiving myself and taking the easier way out? Even though I will add to the force of sin in the world, is there no other possible solution? Catholic theology with such a theory of compromise could better speak to the reality of the world as we know it. Such a theory recognizes the truth in many of the dilemmas brought forth by the situationists, but at the same time the theory of compromise looks beyond the predicament of the individual conscience to the social reality of the total situation.

Notes for Chapter 6

1.

Joseph Fletcher, *Situation Ethics: The New Morality* (West-minster Press, 1966), 64-66; Paul L. Lehmann, *Ethics in a Christian Context* (Harper and Row, 1963), 124-132.

2.

Father Francis J. Connell could accept the conclusions of Fletcher and Lehmann on truth telling because Father Connell defines a lie in relation to the other's right to the truth. See Francis J. Connell C.SS.R., *More Answers to Today's Moral Problems*, ed. Eugene V. Witzel C.S.V. (The Catholic University of America Press, 1965), 124. In a certain sense Professor Fletcher is too absolute and not enough of a situationist! Fletcher says that a particular action (speaking what is not in conformity with what is in the mind) is always lying. However, such an action is lying only when it violates my neighbor's right to truth in a given situation.

3.

Fletcher, 17-39. Situationalism or contexualism is a broad term that describes in general those ethicians who deny the existence of absolute, universal norms of conduct. However, there are many different types of situationists. The present chapter deals almost exclusively with the situation ethics proposed by Joseph Fletcher.

4.

Fletcher, 18-22; 75-77; Josef Fuchs S.J., *Natural Law* (Sheed and Ward, 1965), 123-162.

5.

Philippe Delhaye, *Permanence du Droit Natural* (Editions Nauwelaerts, Louvain, 1960), 10-21.

6.

I-II, q. 94, a. 4.

7.

Jacques Maritain, *The Rights of Man and Natural Law* (Charles Scribner's Sons, 1943), 62.

8.
Columba Ryan O.P., "The Traditional Concept of Natural Law: An Investigation," in *Light on the Natural Law*, ed. Illtud Evans O.P. (Helicon, 1965), 33.
9.
Fuchs, 4-6.
10.
Jacques Jullien, "Nature et culture: Droit naturel ou droit culturel?" *Supplément de La Vie Spirituelle* No. 78 (Septembre 1966), 499, maintains that *Gaudium et Spes* never speaks of natural law as such *(droit naturel)*. However, there are some references to natural law in the document; e.g., n. 74 and n. 79.
11.
Fletcher, 79, 80 and most of Chapter VI, 103-119.
12.
Fletcher, 58.
13.
Fletcher, 42.
14.
Harvey Cox, *The Secular City* (Macmillan, 1965), 192-204.
15.
P. Knauer S. J., "La détermination du bien et du mal morale par le principe du double effet," *Nouvelle Revue Théologique* 87 (1965), 356-375; W. Van der Marck O.P., *Love and Fertility* (Sheed and Ward, London, 1965), 35-63.
16.
Archbishop Denis E. Hurley, "A New Moral Principle," *The Furrow* 17 (1966), 619-622.
17.
See Piet Schoonenberg S.J., *Man and Sin* (University of Notre Dame Press, 1965).

The Mixed Marriage Promises

Chapter Seven

On March 18, 1966, the Sacred Congregation for the Doctrine of the Faith issued an Instruction on mixed marriages.[1] The Instruction modified the legislation found in the Code of Canon Law. According to the Code, the Church most severely condemns mixed marriages, and such marriages are forbidden by divine law where there is danger to the faith of the Catholic spouse or to the faith of any of the children (Canon 1060). The Church grants a dispensation from the impediment of mixed religion (mixed religion concerns a marriage of a Catholic with another baptized person) only for a just and grave cause, provided the promises are signed, and there is moral certitude that the promises will be kept (Canon 1061).

The *cautiones* or promises in the universal law of the Church are two: the non-Catholic promises to remove from the Catholic partner the danger of perversion to his faith; and both partners promise to baptize and raise all the children in the Catholic faith. Canonists have usually taught that the *cautiones* are the way in which the Church safeguards the divine law obligation to bring up all the children as Catholics.[2] The *cautiones* were regularly to be given in writing. The same legislation applied to marriages between a Catholic and a nonbaptized person (Canon 1071).

EVOLUTION OF THE NEW LEGISLATION

The Instruction of March 18, 1966, was generally expected as a result of the deliberations of Vatican II. The antecedents of the present Instruction are most interesting.[3] The Conciliar Commission on the Discipline of the Sacraments received from the preparatory commission six schemata on marriage. After the first session of the Council, the Coordinating Commission reduced the six schemata on marriage to one schema. The Commission on the Sacraments then proposed a schema containing a prooemium, 5 chapters, and a concluding pastoral instruction on the preparation for marriage. The chapter on mixed marriages was to be worked out with the assistance of the Conciliar Commission on the Doctrine of Faith and Morals and the Secretariate for Christian Unity. A committee involving all three commissions approved the chapter on mixed marriages on May 18, 1963. On July 19, 1963, the entire schema was sent to the bishops of the world, who were to make their recommendations and animadversions.

However, on January 23, 1964, the Coordinating Commission instructed the Conciliar Commission on the Sacraments to reduce the schema on marriage to a *votum* or series of recommendations to adapt canonical discipline to the needs of the times in the areas of matrimonial impediments, mixed marriages, the canonical form, and marriage processes. The Commission then examined the communications from the

Fathers of the Council in the light of its new mandate. The *votum* which attempted to enunciate the general guidelines for the future revision of the Code of Canon Law in these matters was sent to the Bishops by Cardinal Cicognani on April 27, 1964. The section dealing with mixed marriages was very brief and merely pointed out that future legislation, within the limits of the divine law, should take into consideration the Conciliar Decree on Ecumenism.[4]

Many of the Bishops replied that the *votum* was too brief and did not provide in a concrete way for the future canonical legislation. The Commission then met and expanded the *votum* especially in the area of mixed marriages. On November 19, 1964, the *votum* on marriage was presented to the Council Fathers in the 126th general congregation. The *votum* makes the following points on the promises in mixed marriages: "In order that canon law in a more opportune way may show greater respect for the condition of persons, in accord with the Decree on Ecumenism and the Declaration on Religious Liberty, safeguarding the demands of divine law, it is desirable above all to make a clear distinction between the regulations governing the marriage of a Catholic partner with a baptized non-Catholic, and the marriage of a Catholic partner with an unbaptized person. Consequently, the following points are to be observed: a) In all mixed marriages, when asking for a dispensation from the impediment, the Catholic party with a grave obligation in conscience will be obliged to make a sincere promise to provide for the Catholic baptism and education of all the children, to the extent that he can *(quantum poterit)*, the non-Catholic party is to be informed about these promises to be made by the Catholic party, and to agree that he or she will not oppose them. . . ."[5]

The question was discussed on November 19 and again on November 20, the last working meeting of the third session of the Council. The short debate showed that a number of influential prelates especially from the Anglo-Saxon countries were not in agreement with the rather liberal stance of the document on the canonical form and the promises in mixed marriages. The debate could not continue because of the lack of time. The Fathers of the Council then voted (1592 *placet;* 427 *non placet;* 5 void) to defer the matter of the *votum* together with their animadversions to the Pope so that he could take care of the matter through the proper channels.[6]

THE INSTRUCTION OF MARCH 18, 1966

The Instruction issued by the Sacred Congregation of the Faith on March 18, 1966, was the final result of what had begun as six schemata on marriage at the first session of the Council. The following changes were made in the legislation concerning the promises made in mixed marriages: 1) The Catholic party alone is to make the explicit promise to provide for the baptism and education of all the children in the Catholic faith. In this way the Catholic party will fulfill the grave obligation of always providing for the baptism and education of the future offspring in the Catholic religion. 2) The non-Catholic party is to be invited to promise sincerely and openly that he will not impede the obligation of the Catholic party. If the non-Catholic party thinks that he cannot make this promise without violating his own conscience, the Ordinary is to refer the case with all its circumstances to the Holy See. 3) Ordinarily, the promises are to be in writing, but the Ordinary can decide either in all cases or in particular cases that the promises do not have to be made in writing. 4) If Catholic education is prevented by the customs and laws of a people, the local Ordinary may dispense from the impediment provided that the Catholic party is ready, insofar as he knows and is able, to do everything possible that all the children to be born will be baptized and educated as Catholics, and that there is certainty of the good will of the non-Catholic party.[7]

The Instruction itself is provisional and will be inserted in the revised Code of Canon Law if it is verified by experience. The implicit recognition of the need for experimental verification of Church law is a most welcome aspect of the present document. Since the document is provisional, theologians and canonists have a duty to study and criticize its provisions. The document definitely attempts to apply the principle of religious liberty and respect the conscience of the non-Catholic partner. The non-Catholic is not asked to promise to bring up the children as Catholics but only promises not to impede the obligation of the Catholic partner. The Instruction also implies that Rome will be willing to do something about the case in which the non-Catholic cannot in conscience make the promise. Likewise, the law now provides for a certain flexibility which was lacking in the older legislation. Greater powers are also given to the local Ordinaries.

However, there are also negative criticisms. The document, which first appeared in *L'Osservatore Romano*, bears internal evidence of haste and/or last minute change. The document is an Instruction of the Sacred Congregation for the Doctrine of the Faith signed by the Pro-Prefect, Cardinal Ottaviani, and the Secretary, Archbishop Parente. However, the document speaks of the "Vatican Council which was summoned by our predecessor of happy memory, Pope John XXIII."[8] Apparently, the document at one time was scheduled to be issued as a *Motu Proprio* from the Pope.

Unfortunately, the Instruction makes no distinction in practice between marriages with other baptized Christians and with nonbaptized persons. Ecumenism and the theology of baptism are two important aspects of contemporary Catholic theology with very practical consequences which cannot be neglected in legislation. The Instruction thus fails to carry out the primary guideline furnished by the *votum* proposed to the Council Fathers on November 19, 1964. The document does contain some flexibility, but more flexibility will be needed in the future. Roman centralization still occupies a more important role than is necessary, since the Ordinaries must send to Rome the cases in which the non-Catholic party cannot in conscience make the promises. The conciliar teaching on collegiality and the national councils of bishops receive no mention in the present legislation.

The Instruction has been criticized by both Protestants and Catholics as not going far enough.[9] The Instruction appears to be a first step which definitely needs further changes.[10] However, the major theological problem for any future legislation of the Church centers on the divine law obligation for the Catholic partner to bring up all the children in the Catholic faith. The Catholic Church must always be true to itself and its mission. In the interest of promoting good will, the Catholic Church can never deny its mission and the truth committed to it. The Catholic Church must clearly propose and answer two questions. 1) What is the divine law obligation on the Catholic partner with regard to the education of the children? 2) What legislation should the Church make in safeguarding the divine obligation or in making other provisions which seem necessary at the present time?

DIVINE LAW OBLIGATION

The question is generally phrased: Is there a divine law obligation for the Catholic partner to baptize and educate all the children of a mixed marriage in the Catholic faith?

Those who assert such an obligation argue from the past teaching of the magisterium. Time after time, papal documents reiterate the divine law obligation to raise all the children as Catholics. It might be true that in certain circumstances the Church has tolerated other arrangements. The Church, however, can never even grant a dispensation from this obligation, for the obligation is from the divine law.[11]

The theological argument affirming such a divine law obligation stems from the fact that the Catholic Church claims to be the true Church of Jesus Christ, and that every Catholic has the right and duty to pass on to his children the Catholic religion. In examining this obligation, commentators point out that the obligation is not a negative obligation, which forbids the placing of intrinsically evil actions. Rather, the obligation is positive and demands the placing of certain actions which bring about the baptism and Catholic education of the children. Theologians point out that a negative obligation is always obliging. The positive divine law obligation, on the other hand, does not demand that the Catholic partner succeed in baptizing and raising the children Catholic, but only that the Catholic party is prepared to do everything possible to attain the Catholic education of all the children. When other more important rights would be involved (e.g., the right to life either of the spouse or the child; the natural right to marry), the Catholic spouse in the face of such circumstances could omit to place the actions required for the spiritual upbringing of the children.[12]

What about the Catholic whose marriage partner feels that he has a right and a duty to raise the children in his faith? In the face of such a conflict, the question cannot be resolved by saying the couple should not marry. Such conflicts are the unfortunate result of the terrible division of Christianity. No solution in this conflict would be satisfactory. Ladislaus Örsy lists five possible solutions. 1) The child is not baptized and not instructed by either parent. 2) The child is baptized, instructed by both parents, but left free to choose his own religion. 3) The children are divided in their religious education. 4) All the children are educated in the same religion. "The conclusion appears inevitable: when the parents are divided in faith, the only reasonable and Christian solution is to have all the children educated in the one religion." 5) Örsy concludes that it would be against her faith for the Church to sanction that the non-Catholic religion should prevail.[13]

Previously, I have argued that there is no divine law obligation to raise all the children of mixed marriages as Catholics.[14] All Catholic theologians must admit that the Catholic Church is the true Church of Christ and that, in general, the spouse has an obligation to pass on his true faith to his children. However, in the question of mixed marriages there are two other principles that must be considered—the principle of religious liberty and the ecumenical principle. The argument affirming such an obligation appears to me to be too unilateral and does not consider the total reality of the situation. Among the conflicting moral truths and principles, I cannot affirm a divine obligation to raise all the children Catholic. Notice that the controversy must center on the word *all*—to educate all the children of mixed marriages as Catholics. I admit a general obligation to raise children as Catholics, but in the light of the other conflicting moral truths, I cannot maintain a strict divine law obligation to raise all the children as Catholics. The argument against the divine law obligation is stronger when the children will be raised as Christians. But there also seem to be cases where no divine law obligation exists because of the principle of religious liberty, even though some of the children might not be raised as Christians.

In practice there might not be too great a difference between the two views. The opinion affirming the divine law

obligation admits situations in which the non-Catholic upbringing of the children may be tolerated. Perhaps, some
theologians and canonists would even be willing to extend
the toleration to include the areas covered by the principle
of religious liberty and the ecumenical principle. The opinion denying the divine law obligation does not speak in
terms of toleration, but precisely because of the complexity
of the reality there seems to be no prior divine law obligation to raise all the children of mixed marriages in the Catholic faith.

DEFICIENCIES IN METHODOLOGY

There seems to be a twofold deficiency in the theological
methodology of those who affirm the divine obligation to
raise all the children Catholic. First, the affirmative view
uses a classicist methodology which is gradually being replaced today by a more historically conscious methodology.
The classicist world view tries to see all reality in terms of
abstract universals which are then applied to concrete reality.
The classicist view abstracts from the particular, the contingent, and the historical, so that it can discover the universal
and eternally true. One then proceeds from the universal to
the particular through the application of laws and casuistry.
Historical mindedness gives much more importance to the
concrete and historical. Historical consciousness does not
deny objectivity, but rather gives greater importance to the
particular and the concrete.[15] An illustration will clarify the
differences.

John Courtney Murray maintains that the Declaration on
Religious Liberty illustrates the movement from classicism
to historical mindedness in theological methodology.[16] A
reflection on the religious liberty controversy shows that the
opposing views were employing different theological methodologies. The classical view started out with an abstract

idea of the perfect society, and then applied this abstraction
to the two societies of the Church and State. This view then
deduced the relationship which should exist between the
two societies. The argument for religious liberty proceeded
differently. Murray started with the experience of the limited state as it exists today and the existing consciousness of
human dignity which demands a freedom of worship and
religion.

The different conclusions come from the different methodologies. Murray himself describes the differing methodologies. The older view: "The problematic of religious liberty
is abstract and simple. It is constructed by two related questions—the moral question of the right of conscience and the
constitutional question."[17] The newer view: "The problematic of religious freedom is concrete and historical. Its
construction begins with a scrutiny of the signs of the time.
Two are decisive. The first is the growth of man's personal
consciousness; the second is the growth of man's political
consciousness."[18] "The question, what is religious freedom,
is not to be answered *a priori* or in the abstract. The fact is
that religious freedom is an aspect of contemporary historical
experience."[19] Notice that the classicist view tried to apply
the universal, abstract ideal in all circumstances. When the
ideal cannot be obtained in the concrete, the classicist view
will tolerate something else. Thus, the classicist view of
Church-State relations spoke of thesis and hypothesis. Murray was always dealing with the concrete historical circumstances and never forced to make such a distinction.

The view affirming the obligation to raise all the children
of mixed marriages in the Catholic faith employs a classicist
methodology. The argument starts from the principle that
the Roman Catholic Church is the true Church of Christ and
that every Catholic is obliged to pass on his faith to his children. All must admit that these principles are true. How-

ever, such a view does not take into account the existing concrete reality.

The classicist view would apply equally well to the Church triumphant or the pilgrim Church. These arguments of the classicist view would apply if there were no religious differences whatsoever. Religious pluralism and even ecclesiological pluralism would not affect these arguments in any way. Notice the abstract and ahistorical character of such reasoning. It is absolutely true, but it does not correspond to the reality of the situation as we know it. Religious pluralism is a fact in our society. Christians, to say nothing of Catholics, are a minority of the world's population. Man today is very much conscious of his individual freedom and dignity to worship God according to the dictates of his own conscience. Abstract arguments based on the true nature of the Church do not come to grips with the objective reality of the situation characterized by pluralism and a consciousness of freedom of worship and religious exercise.

Likewise, the classicist view fails to give any real significance to the ecumenical aspect of contemporary reality.[20] The Catholic Church admits that it is not yet perfect. The Church is the pilgrim Church which is constantly trying to respond better to the call of Christ. (Notice that the classicist world view will naturally have a greater reluctance to admit change and growth.) The pilgrim Church does not have all the attributes of the Church triumphant. The magisterium no longer equates the true Church of Christ with the Roman Catholic Church. The Constitution on the Church (n.8) merely says that the true Church of Christ subsists in the Roman Catholic Church.

Other Christian communities are being recognized as Churches. The Roman Catholic Church does claim to have a greater institutional fullness, but the Catholic Church cannot claim to have a monopoly on the Holy Spirit or even a greater interior life in the *koinonia* of the Spirit than other Christian churches. The classicist view seems to assume that all men are called to the Roman Catholic Church. However, in the light of present historical reality it seems impossible to sustain an effective call by God to all individuals to the Roman Catholic Church. De facto, some men today are not called to the Roman Catholic Church. I cannot exclude the fact that some children of mixed marriages are called by God to be raised in other Christian Churches. At least, all must admit that an upbringing as a good Christian in a Church other than the Catholic Church can never constitute a "perversion" or bring about irreparable harm to the child concerned.

Theology today emphasizes the importance of baptism as the entrance rite into the Christian community. The baptism of most other Christian Churches truly makes children sons of the Father. Christian marriage itself might have an important signifying function in the present situation. Marriage signifies the relationship between Christ and his Church. Theology teaches that the ministers of the sacrament are the baptized couple themselves. A mixed marriage is a real sign of the divided Church as it does exist today. The problem of the religious education of the children would partake of the same sign of unity and division which marks the Church of Christ today.

A classicist methodology necessarily makes a distinction between the ideal or abstract and the real. In Church-State theory, the classicist view spoke of the ideal or thesis and the hypothesis in which some other arrangement could be tolerated. So too in the question of the divine obligation to raise all the children of mixed marriages in the Catholic faith, the classicist view must admit circumstances in which the opposite is tolerated. The classicist methodology does not seem to come to grips with the objective, historical reality of the present situation. At best, it tolerates what does not cohere with its *a priori* worldview. In the present question the classicist methodology completely ignores the very important realities of religious liberty and ecumenical ecclesiology. A more historically conscious methodology takes into consideration all the aspects of reality as it exists here and now. In the light of the total reality of the complex situation it seems impossible to establish a divine law obligation to raise all the children of mixed marriages in the Catholic religion.

LEGALISM

Legalism is a second methodological deficiency in the argument affirming the divine obligation to raise all the children of mixed marriages in the Catholic faith. Note well that theology must always distinguish between true obligations and legalism. The existence of obligations and the insistence on them does not constitute legalism. Legalism, however, endeavors to spell out in advance and know beforehand exactly what will happen. Legalism is closely associated with a classicist world view and methodology. The problem is decided by the application of a law which is always obliging, at least with regard to the effort that a person must expend. Legalism, as used here, is more of a tendency and an attitude than a system. Notice the approach that has been taken. In the conflict of conscience arising from the education of the children, all the different possibilities are listed. Then the various choices are considered and ruled out, so that only one possibility remains. Then the possibility of education of all the children in the same faith is decided by the obligation to raise all the children in the Catholic faith.

Complicated problems cannot be solved by the unilateral application of just one principle. In the face of conflicting principles, the ultimate answer must be left to the prudent judgment of the individuals involved. Too often in the past, Catholic moral theology has neglected the virtue of prudence. But complicated problems admit of no airtight, *a priori* solutions. Perhaps in some circumstances other possibilities for deciding the education of the children might work out. One just cannot exclude from the beginning all these different possibilities. Responsibility must be left with the conscientious individuals themselves to find a creative solution to the problem.

Mixed marriages are always going to cause problems; there can be no *a priori* solution which can always be applied. In an earlier and older society, life was structured mostly from the top down. People lived their lives and made their decisions according to laws. However, today most of life exists outside the pale of law. Law only provides the minimum of public order necessary for man to exercise his creativity and individual responsibility. Law in an older society had a much greater role to play, while personal initiative and creativity had a greatly reduced role. The legalistic mentality still seems to give too prominent a role to the place of law in the life of the Christian. It seems to me more in keeping with reality to speak of a prudent decision of the individual keeping in mind all the obligations present, rather than speak of a divine law which is always obliging, although in some circumstances the opposite may be tolerated.

Sooner or later the legalistic attitude has the problem of explaining why the law does not seem to apply in some circumstances. Even the present Instruction admits in principle that sometimes another solution to the problem has to be tolerated. In those circumstances, theologians affirming a divine obligation must then distinguish between the *de facto* placing of the acts of education and the will to place such acts. However, such a distinction bears the stamp of the unreal. Can there really be a true obligation in those cases?

What is an obligation to have the will to do everything possible to achieve the purpose? Would it not be better to admit that in certain cases one cannot say for sure which of the conflicting obligations should be followed? It seems arrogant and unreal to maintain that we can always know in advance what should be done in a very complicated situation.

My conclusion is that in the light of political and religious pluralism, the right to religious liberty, and the reality of ecumenical ecclesiology, it is impossible to affirm an *a priori* divine law obligation to raise all the children of mixed marriages in the Catholic faith. The opinion affirming such an obligation seems to labor under a twofold methodological deficiency—a classicist world view and a legalistic attitude. One cannot deny the true nature of the Church and the right and duty of the Catholic parent to educate his child in this most important of all areas. If the non-Catholic partner can agree to the Catholic education of the children without violating his own conscience, then there would be a "divine law" obligation to raise all the children Catholic. I object to the attempt to give an *a priori* divine law solution to such a complex reality. In some cases the ultimate solution must be left to the prudent decision of the persons concerned. The difficulties involved in coming to a responsible decision in a given situation merely mirror the difficulties existing in mixed marriages because of the pilgrim nature of the Church and the division existing in Christianity.

Many objections come to mind. What about the traditional teaching of the magisterium about the divine law obligation of raising all the children of mixed marriages in the Catholic faith? There were similar documents of the magisterium concerning religious liberty. The situation has changed today precisely because of the contemporary consciousness of religious liberty and the ecumenical principle.

A more historically minded methodology can solve the problem created by the past teaching of the magisterium in this area just as it did in the area of religious liberty.

What about the rights of a child to be raised in the Catholic religion of one of his parents? Since faith is a free gift of God, one cannot speak about rights to the Catholic faith.[21] Is invoking the ecumenical principle an example of false irenicism?[22] Are theologians invoking the ecumenical principle just to ingratiate themselves with the Protestants even to the extent of sacrificing truths of the faith? The ecumenical principle is not based simply on a desire not to offend Protestants. Catholic theologians can never deny that the Roman Catholic Church is the true Church of Christ. However, the ecumenical principle is based on solid theological teachings—the pilgrim state of the Church, the existence of other Christian communities that are churches, the presence of the Holy Spirit in such communities, the importance of baptism, the meaning of marriage. The Catholic Church and the individual Catholic can still hold that the Catholic Church is the one, true Church of Christ and at the same time deny a divine law obligation to raise all the children of mixed marriages in the Catholic faith.

ROLE OF CHURCH LAW

What is the role of the Church in the question of the mixed marriage promises? One must carefully distinguish between the role of the Church and the role of Church law. Church law is not synonymous with the whole Church. Too often in the past the Church has relied too exclusively on law. The Church always has the duty of proclaiming and safeguarding the divine law. Likewise, the Church must promote the good of its members and help them to live their Christian lives in the world. The teaching and living Church constantly witnesses to the importance of the faith, the true nature of the Catholic Church, and the general obligation of parents to educate their children in the Catholic faith. But likewise the Church must teach the principle of religious liberty and the ecumenical principle. The Church must especially provide this assistance for people who might be contemplating marriage. Education and witness must always occupy a higher place than law in the pedagogy and help that the Church tries to give to its members. The Church as the community of salvation in history has learned some of the difficulties connected with mixed marriages and must communicate such experience to all its members. The Church has also learned the danger of impulsive marriages especially on the part of the young, and must make every effort that its younger members will profit from such experience.

What should be the specific role of Church law with regard to the promises in a mixed marriage? I think it would be better if there were no specific legislation about the need for making promises in certain situations. The Church should rather expend its efforts in a positive teaching of all the obligations involved on a Catholic partner in a mixed marriage, especially when the non-Catholic partner cannot agree in conscience to have all the children raised in the Catholic faith.

Perhaps in the past the Church has put too much trust in the pedagogical value of positive Church law. The law of the Church severely prohibiting mixed marriages really did not accomplish its intended purpose of discouraging mixed marriages. Is the law of mixed marriages accomplishing its purpose in view of the following statistics of mixed marriages which occur outside the Catholic Church: in Holland, 80%; in Switzerland, 58%?[23] Pastoral experience points out that many people will make the promises just to be married in the Church, but they will not bother to fulfill them. Experience also shows that there is no substitute for the deep faith of the partners themselves, and generally the faith of the partners determines the upbringing of the children. In the past, the law on mixed marriages has not of itself been that effective in making Catholics cognizant of their obligations and in helping Catholics to fulfill their obligations.

The practical difficulty in making Church laws for the promises in mixed marriages is the difficulty of discerning what is the divine law obligation in a particular situation. Many times only the prudential conscience judgment of the individual can tell. Law has a difficulty in legislating for so many contingent circumstances. If there were a law demanding the promises in certain circumstances, it would have to admit of exceptions, dispensations, and privileges because of the complicated reality of the situation. In practice such dispensations become so routine that the law loses whatever pedagogical value it had for the individual person. There are even some indications now that the cases in which the non-Catholic party cannot agree in conscience to the Catholic upbringing of the children will be handled in a routine fashion by Rome. The problem with any system of permissions, dispensations, etc. is that the person best qualified to make the judgment is the person on the scene and not the local or Roman curia. If the higher authority does handle the matter routinely, then in practice the final decision is made by the person himself when he asks for the dispensation or permisison. It seems to me that any laws demanding the promises but allowing for dispensations and permissions are bound to prove unsuccessful in practice.

The question of the faith of the children should simply be left with the conscience of the individual Catholic and his spouse after the Church has done everything possible to to instruct them on all aspects of the question. Perhaps in a particular region or for a particular class of people (e.g. youthful marriages), special legislation might be helpful.

However, I am confining my argument to the principle that there should be no general Church legislation about promises in mixed marriages.

No one can deny the complexity of the problem of mixed marriages. No legislation is ever going to solve the problem of mixed marriages, since mixed marriages merely reflect the problems of a pluralistic society and a divided Christianity. However, the very complexity of the problem argues against the divine law obligation of the Catholic partner to raise all the children in the Catholic faith and also argues against the possible effectiveness of any particular Church legislation.

Notes for Chapter 7

1.
Acta Apostolicae Sedis, 58 (March 31, 1966) , 235-239.
2.
Felix M. Cappello S.I., *De Sacramentis; Vol. V: De Matrimonio*, 7th ed. (Marietti, Rome, 1961) , n. 309.
3.
The history of the proposed conciliar document on marriage is sketched in the Appendix of the *Votum* sent to all the bishops on April 27, 1964.
4.
"Quo opportunius condicioni personarum consulatur, ad matrimonia mixta quod attinet, salvis exigentiis iuris divini, leges canonicae de impedimentis mixtae religionis et disparitatis cultus accommodentur attentis peculiaribus normis quae Sacrosanta Synodus statuit de Oecumenismo."
5.
The original Latin test is as follows: "Ad matrimonia mixta quod attinet, quo opportunius, salvis exigentiis iuris divini, leges canonicae condicioni personarum consulant, ad mentem Decreti de Oecumenismo necnon declarationis de libertate religiosa, optandum est praecipue, ut separentur praescripta circa matrimonium partis catholicae cum parte baptizata non catholica et partis catholicae cum parte non

baptizata. Dein vero sequentia serventur: a) In omnibus matrimoniis mixtis ad impetrandam dispensationem impedimenti, pars catholica, graviter onerata conscientia, promissionem sinceram praestare debebit se, in quantum poterit, baptismum et educationem catholicam universae prolis esse curaturam. De his promissionibus a parte catholica faciendis, partem non catholicam (tempestive) moneri oportebit, atque constare eam illis non repugnare; item certior pars non catholica fiat de finibus et proprietatibus essentialibus matrimonii a neutro contrahente excludendis." An English translation with some inaccuracies may be found in, Xavier Rynne, *The Third Session* (Farrar, Straus and Giroux, 1965), 229, 230.
6.
"Il Concilio Vaticano II: Notiziario n. 65," *La Civilta Cattolica*, 116, Vol. 3 (1965), 476-485.
7.
The complete translation of the pertinent parts of the Instruction from the N.C.W.C. translation may be helpful for the reader:

I.   1. It should always be kept in mind that danger to the faith is to be warded off from the Catholic spouse and that the education of the child in the Catholic religion must be cared for diligently (cf. Canon 1060).

2. The local Ordinary or the pastor of the Catholic party will take care to inculcate in grave words the obligation of always providing for the baptism and education of the future offspring in the Catholic religion. The fulfillment of this obligation will be assured by the explicit promise or guarantee made by the same Catholic party.

3. The non-Catholic party with due respect, but in a clear manner, is certainly to be informed of the Catholic teaching about the dignity of matrimony and especially about its chief qualities which are unity and indissolubility.

The grave obligation of the Catholic spouse to guard, preserve, profess his (her) own faith and to baptize and educate in that faith the offspring that may be born must be made known to the same non-Catholic party.

Since this obligation must be safeguarded the non-Catholic entering marriage is to be invited to promise sincerely and openly that he will in no way impede this obligation. If, however, the non-Catholic party thinks that he cannot make this promise without violating his own conscience, the Ordinary is to refer the case with all its circumstances to the Holy See.

4. Although by the ordinary law these promises are to be given in writing, it is, however, in the power of the Ordinary to decide, either in general or in individual cases, whether this promise of the Catholic party or the non-Catholic party or of both is to be given in writing or not, and likewise to determine how this is to be entered in the marriage records.

II. If in some place, as sometimes happens in some regions, the Catholic education of the child is prevented not so much by the choice of the spouses as by the laws and customs of the people which those entering marriage are forced to obey, the local Ordinary, when everything is carefully considered, can dispense from this impediment provided that the Catholic party is ready, insofar as he knows and is able, to do everything that every child that will be born be baptized and educated as a Catholic and that there is certainty of the good will of the non-Catholic party. In making these concessions the Church is led by the hope that the civil laws contrary to human liberty, such as those which forbid the Catholic education of the child or the practice of the Catholic religion, will be abolished and that so the natural law will prevail in these matters.

8.

The above phrase appeared in the Instruction as published in *L'Osservatore Romano*, March 19, 1966. The official version published later in *A.A.S.*, 58 (1966), 236, corrected the original error and reads "... Concilium Oecumenicum Vati-

canum II, quod idcirco a Summo Pontifice Ioanne XXIII, fel. rec., indictum est . . ."
9.
E.g., Peter Hebblethwaite S.J., "Rome and Canterbury Now," *The Month*, 35 (May, 1966), 294-296; Gregory Baum, "Mixed Marriage—An Ecumenical Issue," *The Ecumenist*, 4 (July-August, 1966), 73-76. The same issue of *The Ecumenist*, 85, 86, gives the reaction of Visser 'T Hooft.
10.
Ladislaus Örsy S.J., "La Recente Istruzione sui Matrimoni Misti," *La Civilta Cattolica*, 117, Vol. 3 (1966), 345-362.
11.
Ladislaus Örsy S.J., "Documenta selecta de educatione religiosa prolis ex matrimonio mixto natae," *Periodica de Re Morali Canonica Liturgica*, 53 (1964), 267-284.
12.
Ladislaus Örsy S.J., "The Religious Education of Children Born from Mixed Marriages," *Gregorianum*, 45 (1964), 739-760; Franz Böckle, "Mixed Marriages: A Roman Catholic View," *Concilium*, Vol. 4, n. 1 (April 1965), 60-63; Richard A. McCormick, S.J., "Notes on Moral Theology," *Theological Studies*, 26 (1965), 649-654.
13.
Örsy, *Gregorianum*, 45 (1964), 748-752. Since this chapter was written, Örsy has published another article on the subject: "Mixed Marriages," *America*, Vol. 117, n. 11 (Sept. 9, 1967), 242-246. Although he has somewhat modified his earlier positions, he still speaks of the "duty to educate all the children in the Catholic faith. . . ." "Note that the Catholic parent is never dispensed from his divine mission, but he has to carry it out with discretion."
14.
Charles E. Curran, *Christian Morality Today* (Fides, 1966), 93-105. I do not intend in this chapter to repeat the arguments I have already developed.
15.
Bernard J. F. Lonergan S.J., *Insight* (Longmans, Green and Co., 1957); also Lonergan, "The Transition from a Classi-

cist World-View to Historical Mindedness," a paper presented to the seminar on The Role of Law in the Church sponsored by the Canon Law Society of America, now published in *Law for Liberty: The Role of Law in the Church Today* (Helicon Press, 1967).
16.
John Courtney Murray S.J., "The Declaration on Religious Freedom," *Concilium*, Vol. 5, n. 2. (May, 1966), 7-10.
17.
John Courtney Murray S.J., *The Problem of Religious Freedom* (Newman, 1965), 7. This book originally appeared as an article in *Theological Studies*, 25 (1964), 503-575.
18.
Murray, 17.
19.
Murray, 22.
20.
Cf., The *Decree on Ecumenism* and parts of the first two chapters of the *Constitution on the Church*.
21.
I have answered these objections more fully in *Christian Morality Today*, 93-105.
22.
"As for the principle of ecumenism adduced by Fr. Curran, I see in the practical concessions made by the Catholic the germ of the very indifferentism he claims was behind earlier documents of the Church." McCormick, *Theological Studies*, 26 (1965), 654.
23.
Bertulf van Leeuwen O.F.M., *Het gemengde huwelijk*, (Van Gorcum, Assen, 1959), 313 ff. The pertinent sociological information is also given in German, French, and English; van Leeuwen, "Législation des mariages mixtes et rapports entre catholiques et protestants," *Social Compass*, XI/2 (1964), 1-12; Joseph Candolfi, "Marriages mixtes en Suisse," *Choisir*, 40 (Février, 1963), 16-18.

Masturbation and
Objectively Grave Matter

Chapter Eight

Manuals of moral theology teach that "direct and perfectly voluntary pollution is always and intrinsically a grave sin."[1] On the level of popular instruction theological nuances disappear; many children are taught that masturbation is always a mortal sin. In the light of recent psychological knowledge, theologians have cautiously been considering the subjective imputability of masturbation.[2] Josef Fuchs very gingerly proposes the general conclusion that "grave subjective guilt is not rarely lacking."[3] The guarded theological conclusion proposed by Fuchs and others has apparently been seeping into confessional practice and popular instruction.[4]

Does the "objectively grave but perhaps not subjectively culpable" solution really correspond to the reality of the question? The purpose of the present chapter is to argue that the act of masturbation does not always involve grave matter. Note well that the essay does not try to prove that masturbation is not sinful or that masturbation can never involve grave sin. The scope of the discussion is very limited: masturbation is not an action which is *ex toto genere suo grave.*

Dialogue with the modern world shows that other Christians, educators, and psychologists do not believe that a single masturbatory act constitutes a serious and grave matter.[5] Even Catholic educators do not view individual masturbatory actions, especially among adolescents, as seriously harmful to the development of the person.[6] The attitude of the vast majority of these people of competent knowledge and good will might be wrong, but Catholic theologians must enter into dialogue with them in the search of truth.

Psychological studies indicate that masturbatory actions are generally symptomatic.[7] Empirical and statistical studies point out that the majority of adolescents go through a more or less prolonged period of masturbatory activity. "We can say without fear of contradiction that the masturbator is the rule, and the abstainer the exception."[8] Such activity does not seem to involve a harmful influence on the maturity and development of the person. Yet Catholic theology teaches that masturbation is intrinsically grave matter; i.e., the act itself is prohibited because in itself it is seriously wrong. Do modern scientific findings seem to contradict the teaching that masturbation is of itself a serious matter? Does the teaching of theologians really come to grips with the intrinsic meaning of masturbation?

Confessional practice indicates that often the masturbator has not broken his relationship of love with God. The prudent confessor judges the general disposition of the penitent on the gospel criterion of union with God and neighbor. Frequently the external signs indicate that the masturbator, especially the adolescent, has not broken his relationship of love with God and neighbor. Since the relationship of love with God should involve some stability, no individual can psychologically be in and out of a profound union of love with God three or four times a week! The "objectively grave —subjectively not culpable" approach offers a good pastoral solution for the priest or confessor. However, theologians must ask the further question: does not the confessional experience of a frequent lack of subjective guilt indicate that the matter itself might not be objectively grave?

There are at least three other major objections to the "objectively grave—subjectively not culpable" approach. (1) Such an approach seems to say that if everything were normal, masturbation would be a mortal sin. The logical conclusion would be that the masturbator does not commit mortal sin because he is not normal! Yet, statistics show that, for the adolescent, masturbation is the rule. (2) Some experts in psychology indicate that the present teaching of always grave matter in masturbation occasions "irrational and excessive guilt."[9] (3) Insistence on the teaching that masturbation always involves grave matter exposes the teaching of the Church to the ridicule of many learned scholars and people of good will.

SIN IN THE THEORY OF THE FUNDAMENTAL OPTION

The precise area of difficulty appears to be the fact that the manuals have considered the act of masturbation in a very static way and completely apart from the person placing the action. Since human life is a continually growing process, any static consideration will be somewhat unreal. Likewise, moral theology can no longer consider the action apart from the person who places the action.[10] In the light of the inadequacies of the manualistic considerations of sin and in the light of a more scriptural and dogmatic concept of sin, theologians are beginning to see the human act and sin in relation to the fundamental option of man.

The theory of the fundamental option is definitely rooted in the teaching of Augustine and especially in St. Thomas' teaching on the last end.[11] According to the Thomistic teaching there are many particular individual choices that a man makes. Some choices, for example, choice of a vocation, are more basic than others. The more fundamental choices guide and direct other individual choices. Ultimately, there are only two possible fundamental options—the love of God or the love of a creature, which in the last analysis is self. Man either chooses God as his ultimate end and directs all his activity toward God, or he chooses self and directs all his activity toward self. A particular individual action has meaning insofar as it makes incarnate and intensifies the fundamental option.

A more existential consideration sees man as an image of God with a twofold freedom—freedom with regard to particular choices (*liberum arbitrium*) ; and a fundamental and existential freedom of option in the profundity of his person. Around this basic and profound freedom man directs and integrates his total personality. Man in the depths of his own existence engages himself for God or for a creature. This project or stance, which man takes for or against God, guides and directs his other activity. Individual actions are seen as the expression of the relationship of love binding the particular person to God. The existential involvement in the depths of the person expresses itself in the individual external action.[12]

The theory of the fundamental option also coheres with a more personalist understanding of grace. Theologians today do not emphasize created grace, but uncreated grace, the relationship of love existing between God and man.[13] God's love for man is creative and expresses itself in his gifts to man. Sin becomes the breaking of this relationship of love with God. Again, the particular action has meaning insofar as it expresses this profound, personal relationship between God and man.

The theological speculations on the fundamental option merely build on the biblical notion of sin, with a special dependence on St. Paul. St. Paul generally uses the singular, *hamartia*, in his reference to sin and distinguishes *hamartia* from transgressions. *Hamartia* is the personified sin that dwells in the heart of man and manifests itself in external actions. The external action has an existential meaning insofar as the action comes from the *hamartia* that dwells in the heart of man. St. Paul divides all men into two classes: these under the law of *hamartia*, who do evil works; and those under the law of the Spirit, who do good works.[14] As the scripture phrases it: the good tree brings forth good fruit, while the evil tree brings forth evil fruit. Theology develops the same idea in the distinction between the state of sin and the state of grace. The person in the state of grace performs good works, whereas the person in the state of sin performs sinful works.

In the theory of the fundamental option, the particular action is seen not in static isolation but in relationship to the development of the person. Such an existential consideration must be balanced by an objective consideration, which views the act in relation to other persons and the total society. The torture of the Inquisition and the cooperation with the Nazis were wrong actions even though the persons involved in such actions may not have broken their fundamental option of love for God. Objectively evil actions may result from subjective limitations and pressures—and not necessarily from a sinful fundamental option.

More important in the present discussion of the fundamental option is the distinction between mortal and venial sin. Generally, moral theology manuals speak of sin as venial, either by reason of the imperfection of the act or by reason of the lightness of the matter. But can only a difference of degree in matter constitute the great difference between mortal and venial sin? According to the theory of the fundamental option, the difference between mortal and venial sin lies in the existential involvement of the subject in a particular action. Mortal sin is an action which involves a fundamental option, whereas venial sin remains a more superficial and peripheral action not involving the core of the person. Bernard Häring insists that Augustine and the scholastic writers maintain that the ultimate difference between mortal and venial sin lies in the imperfection of the act, i.e., the subjective involvement in the action.[15]

The following arguments seem to bolster the fact that the difference between mortal and venial sin consists in the personal involvement in the action.[16] (1) Traditional scholastic teaching maintains that Adam and the angels could not commit a mere venial sin. The pure spirit and man without sin must necessarily involve themselves totally in the actions they perform. (2) Early scholastic speculation defined venial sin by reason of the imperfection of the act, especially in considering the first indeliberate motions of the appetite which are not completely under the full control of reason. (3) Some saints believed that they would break their relationship with God even over rather small matters. Perhaps exaggerations in the lives of saints have come from poor hagiography; but for two people in a close union of love even a seemingly insignificant matter has great importance for their relationship. (4) Although holding to a reciprocity between matter and form, scholastic theology has maintained that the form gives meaning and intelligibility to the matter. (5) The theory of the final option in the moment of death also presupposes that mortal and venial sin differ by reason of the imperfection of the act.[17]

What then is the value of the distinction between grave and light matter? Such a distinction has meaning only as a presumptive guideline and not as a metaphysical norm.[18] Grave matter is such that ordinarily a subject will engage the depths of his person in the action. Light matter is such that ordinarily the person does not involve the core of his personality in the action. Light matter indicates that the action will generally be superficial and peripheral—and not a fundamental choice. Many of our daily actions are merely peripheral and do not completely involve our persons. The distinction between grave and light matter is not iron-clad, but only a presumptive guideline. *A fortiori*, the expression *ex toto genere suo grave* loses much of its absolute character.

Likewise, theologians should carefully distinguish between grave and light sin and grave and light matter. No one should say blasphemy (in the abstract) is a grave sin, but rather that it is grave matter. A theologian, when discussing an action in the abstract, can speak of the gravity of matter, but it would be better to avoid speaking of gravity of sin. Sin refers to the relationship between God and man. ·

But our investigation must go one step further. Is there a valid presumption that masturbation is an action which is always grave matter (*ex toto genere suo grave*)? Does the act of masturbation so involve the core of the person that man generally makes a fundamental option with regard to it? The empirical evidence cited in the first portion of this paper indicates that masturbation, especially among adolescents, does not involve a fundamental option. Since masturbatory activity is symptomatic, it can have many different meanings. The ambiguous nature of masturbation argues against the theory that masturbation always involves grave matter. It would seem impossible to conclude, even as a presumption, that every masturbatory act as such involves a fundamental option.

A REEVALUATION OF THE TEACHING OF THE MANUALS

The basic assertion of this paper is that the act of masturbation is not always objectively grave matter. In the preceding section I have tried to prove the assertion in the light of
the theory of the fundamental option. Now I will endeavor
to show that the basic assertion is an application of the best
insights of the traditional Thomistic teaching to what contemporary man knows about masturbation. The Church,
throughout its teaching, has formulated a distinction between mortal and venial sin. However, the philosophical distinction as it exists in the theology textbooks stems from a
Thomistic interpretation and has never been solemnly
taught as such by the Church.[19] Recently, a different theory
and definition of mortal sin has been proposed.[20] Consequently, a theologian should not exaggerate the dogmatic
value of the understanding of the philosophical difference
between venial and mortal sin.

St. Thomas tried to find the difference between mortal
and venial sin in the acts themselves and not in the punishments; the diverse punishments are effects of the acts. Mortal
sin is *contra caritatem, contra finem, contra ordinem;* whereas
venial sin is *praeter caritatem, praeter finem, praeter ordinem.*[21] Thomas also noted the difference on the basis of repa-
rability. Mortal sin destroys the ordering to the ultimate
end, which is the fundamental principle of the spiritual life.
Consequently, there remains nothing intrinsic in man which
can repair the damage of mortal sin. Since venial sin involves
a deordination of means (and not end), the ultimate principle of the spiritual life remains and can repair the damage
of venial sin (*I II*, q. 88, a.1, corp.) .

Thomas does speak about sins *ex genere suo grave* and *ex
genere suo leve.* But the determination of the objective
gravity depends on whether the object itself is repugnant to

charity, which orders man to his ultimate end. Consequently, a sin is mortal *ex genere suo* if it is against the love of God (e.g., blasphemy, perjury) or against the love of neighbor (e.g., homicide, adultery) . (*I II*, q. 88, a.2, corp.) Elsewhere, Thomas also defined mortal sin *ex genere suo* in terms of the object which is opposed to the ultimate end, charity.[22] In discussing particular sins, Thomas refers to the same criterion—mortal sin *ex genere suo* exists if the object is against love of God and neighbor.[23]

With regard to sins against chastity, Thomas applies the same criterion: "Mortal sin is every sin which is committed directly against the life of man" (*II II*, q. 154, a.2, corp.) . Fornication is a mortal sin because of the harm such an action does to the child who might be born of such a union. With regard to pollution, Thomas merely mentions that it is against that natural order of venereal actions of the human species (*II II*, q. 154, a.12, corp.) . Since God is the author of nature, Thomas concludes that an injury is done to God when the order of nature is broken (*II II*, q. 154, a.12, ad 1[um]) . Many theologians today propose basically the same reason for the gravity of masturbation—"a substantial inversion of an order of very great importance."[24]

The concept of matter *ex toto genere suo grave* as enunciated in the manuals of moral theology stems from the Thomistic teaching. For example, Dom Lottin, one of the best of the Thomistic moralists, describes mortal sins *ex toto genere suo grave* as those which "directly offend God or a divine attribute (infidelity, heresy, hatred of God, idolatry, blasphemy, etc.) ; those in which grave matter is indivisible (homicide, violation of the Eucharistic fast) ; those which if they were only forbidden under penalty of venial sin would be too easily committed (direct violation of the seal of confession, all voluntary *luxuria* even incomplete) ."[25] The third category, which includes *luxuria*, seems to betray the basic Thomistic note of realism. Sin can never be conceived as a penalty. The Church cannot use sin as civil rulers use penalties to force compliance with laws. Sin is the reality of man's breaking his relationship of love with God and neighbor. The fundamental attitude of Thomistic morality is the intrinsic nature of morality—something is forbidden because it itself is wrong. If the object itself, even in its widest extension, is not opposed to charity, then the matter cannot be grave. Perhaps the underlying reason for placing *luxuria* in such a category is that if man were able to enjoy these other sexual actuations without mortal sin, then he would never embrace marriage. Thus the good of the species would be greatly harmed. Another reason for making *luxuria* a mortal sin according to the category proposed by Lottin might be the harm that society would suffer from the frequency of such sins if they were forbidden "only under penalty of venial sin." Such reasoning does not appear to be conclusive. Consequently, the reason for the gravity of sexual sins as proposed by Lottin does not appear to be valid. The only valid criterion for determining grave matter is the Thomistic teaching—grave matter is that which is opposed to charity. Can one prove that masturbation is *contra caritatem* in the form of a substantial inversion of an important order of nature?

What do the theology manuals teach about the intrinsic malice and gravity of masturbation? Theologians in the past have not been in agreement about the ultimate malice of masturbation. Some argue that the voluntary frustration of semen is intrinsically and gravely evil. Others place the formal malice in the complete venereal pleasure outside the marital act. Others find the malice of masturbation in the danger to the species, for men would not enter marriage and procreate children if masturbation were permitted. In the recent theological literature there appears to be a growing consensus that masturbation is intrinsically a grave evil because it is a substantial inversion of an order of the greatest importance. [26]

Theologians must ask a precise question: does the single act of masturbation constitute a substantial inversion of a very important order of nature? Five reasons seem to prove that a single masturbatory action does not constitute a substantial inversion of a very important order.

(1) Older theologians have had too narrow and unilateral an understanding of masturbatory activity. From a purely biological and physiological viewpoint, masturbation may constitute a substantial inversion of sexual actuation. However, a total human consideration embraces much more than the mere biological emission of semen. The psychological understanding of masturbation does not seem to warrant the severity with which moral theologians speak about masturbation. Masturbation as a total human action does not seem that important or serious.

(2) Consideration of the gravity of masturbation has again been too narrow and unilateral in concentrating almost exclusively on the relationship of sexuality with procreation.[27] Sexuality must also be considered in relationship to other persons and to the individual himself. Masturbation might indicate a narcissistic behavior pattern, a period of temporary stress, or a developing stage of adolescent sexuality. Since masturbation is a complex human reality involving a multiplicity of relationships, the moralist distorts reality by considering masturbation solely in terms of procreation.

(3) Inadequate physiological knowledge merely heightened the unilateral emphasis on the procreational and biological aspects. Since science thought that semen was the primary and only active agent in procreation, the arguments against masturbation stressed the teleology of the semen. Only in the last century did theologians begin to realize a

consideration based on the teleology of the semen was too unilateral because it did not explain the reality of female masturbation.[28] However, a disordinate stress on the teleology of semen has contributed to a misjudgment about the seriousness of masturbation.

Only since the invention of the microscope in the seventeenth century has science gradually acquired a better understanding of the process of human reproduction. Just a few centuries ago scientists themselves thought that semen was the only active element in human reproduction. The very name semen—seed—indicates that the woman merely supplied the fertile field in which the seed developed into a human person. Nothing was known of the total female reproductive system and the process of fertilization through union of the ovum and sperm. Semen thus took on a greatly exaggerated importance because it was thought to be so closely connected with human life. Contemporary science realizes the greatly reduced importance of semen because of the prodigality of nature in giving the male so many million sperm and also because fertilization requires that the sperm penetrate the ovum. Thus the contemporary theologian understands the exaggerated importance attributed to human semen by the authors of the classical works in moral theology.

(4) It does not seem that a single masturbatory action can constitute a substantial inversion of an order of very great importance. Perhaps in the past theologians have illegitimately transferred to the individual act the importance that belongs to the sexual faculty.[29] I am not saying that individual actions are never important; but in the total consideration of masturbation, individual actions do not always constitute a substantial inversion of human sexuality.

(5) Most contemporary theologians and educators recognize that in the past there was an overemphasis on sexual sins. The overly spiritual heresies from Gnosticism to Jansenism

have warped our understanding of human sexuality. The inadequate and distorted notions of the past have contributed to the importance and gravity attached to individual masturbatory actions. A word of caution, however, is in order. Today, when many are espousing the "Playboy philosophy," Catholic teaching must uphold the dignity and importance of human sexuality. However, Catholic teaching must avoid the temptation of overreacting to laxist, and ultimately inhuman, notions of sexuality.

POSSIBLE OBJECTIONS

What about the traditional teaching of the Church? There appears to be no traditional, authoritative, unchangeable teaching of the Church that masturbation is always objectively grave matter. Remember that the philosophical distinction between mortal and venial sin and the question of matter *ex toto genere suo grave* did not exist before St. Thomas. With regard to masturbation itself, there is no conclusive proof that scripture mentions the malice (let alone the always grave matter) of masturbation.[30] The fathers of the Church are practically silent on the simple question of masturbation. No mention is made of masturbation with regard to the public penance in the early Church. More frequent mention of masturbation appears in the penitentials.[31]

The authoritative interventions of the magisterium before the present century never explicitly teach that the matter of masturbation is always grave; but such teachings do imply, at least in general, the gravity of the sin of masturbation. The letter of Leo IX (1054) considers masturbation in the context of the promotion of clerics to orders and their reinstatement in orders following penance.[32] The Holy Office under Alexander VII (1655-1656) condemned as a group 45 propositions as being *"ut minime scandalosae."* Proposition 24 reads: *"Mollities, sodomia et bestialitas sunt peccata eiusdem speciei infimae; ideoque suffict dicere in confessione se procurasse pollutionem"* (*D.S.* 2044). The condemnation does imply that masturbation is necessary matter for confession. The Holy Office, under Innocent XI, in 1679, condemned a group of 65 propositions: *"sicut iacent, ut minimum tamquam scandalosae et in praxi perniciosae"* (*D.S.* 2166). Proposition 49 states: *"Mollities jure naturae prohibita non est. Unde, si Deus eam non interdixisset, saepe esset bona et aliquando obligatoria sub mortali"* (*D.S.* 2149). The precise object of the condemnation might only be the fact that on occasions there could be a *sub gravi* command to masturbate!

The interventions of the present century have concentrated especially on masturbation for medical reasons. Despite interventions of the Holy Office (July 24, 1929) and allocutions of Pope Pius XII,[33] one respected theologian maintains that "masturbation" for the purpose of seminal analysis is probably licit.[34] At least the proposing of such an opinion indicates that the interventions of the magisterium in this regard do not involve an irreparable commitment.

In the whole question of the gravity of masturbation (to say nothing of *ex toto genere suo grave*) the official magisterium of the Church has never even come close to an irreparable teaching. Perhaps the strongest argument from the teaching of the Church comes from the constant teaching of catechisms since the time of Trent. However, this teaching was always modified on the existential plane by the application of the principles governing the necessity of knowledge and the necessity of advertence for mortal sin. Consequently, in the light of a better understanding of the matter of masturbation, it could be that masturbation is no longer considered a matter which is always and necessarily grave.

The teaching on parvity of matter directly and immediately concerns incomplete sexual actuation or pleasure outside marriage and not the question of masturbation. In 1612, Claudius Aquaviva, the general of the Society of Jesus, severely forbade the Jesuits to hold the possibility of light matter in imperfect sexual pleasure, but the condemnation was in practice and not necessarily in theory.[35] In 1659 the *Revisores* of the Society of Jesus admitted that the opinion favoring the possibility of light matter was still extrinsically probable and not condemned by the Church.[36] Despite some interventions on the subject by Clement VIII and Paul V, as well as Proposition 40 condemned by Alexander VII, G. J. Waffelaert avoided making a judgment on the matter because in practice there seems to be no difference between the theory of parvity of matter and the distinction between venereal pleasure and sensible pleasure. Those who make such a distinction between sexual and sensible pleasure can come to the same practical solutions as those who hold parvity of matter.[37] The above remarks make no attempt at being a complete consideration of the question of parvity of matter, since such a question does not directly effect the proposed theory on the gravity of masturbation. However, the teaching on parvity of matter must also be rethought in the light of the fundamental option.[38]

In conclusion, moral theologians must become more aware of their proper function. In the past, we moralists spent most of our time interpreting the documents of the magisterium for the Christian people. Today the Vatican Council and theologians are beginning to recognize the importance of the experience of Christian people.[39] Theologians must also interpret the experience of Christian people for the magisterium. Theologians, likewise, cannot merely repeat older formulae and conclusions. Previous teachings must be examined in the light of the circumstances of the times in which they were formed. In the question of masturbation, newer scientific knowledge of the psychological and physical reality of masturbation, better theological insights, and the experience of Christians and other men of good will argue for a change in the former teaching that masturbation always involves grave matter.

Notes for Chapter 8

1.
Marcellino Zalba S.J., *Theologiae Moralis Summa*, Vol. II (Matriti, Biblioteca de Autores Cristianos 1953), 366.
2.
See Frederick Von Gagern, *The Problem of Onanism* (Mercier Press, Cork, 1955), pp. 39-94, and also the articles by Angermair and Fleckenstein in the Appendix; P. Snoeck S.J., "Masturbation and Grave Sin," *New Problems in Medical Ethics*, Vol. I, ed. Dom Peter Flood O.S.B. (Mercier Press, Cork, 1962), 46-57; George Hagmaier C.S.P., and Robert Gleason S.J., *Counselling the Catholic* (Sheed and Ward, 1959), 73-93 and 215-227; John C. Ford S.J., and Gerald Kelly S.J., *Contemporary Moral Theology*, Vol. I (Newman Press, 1958), 174-201. Further bibliography is found in these references.
3.
Josephus Fuchs S.J., *De Castitate et Ordine Sexuali*, 3rd. ed. (Editrice Università Gregoriana, Roma, 1963), 181.
4.
Richard A. McCormick S.J., "The Priest and Teen-Age Sexuality," *Homiletic and Pastoral Review* 65 (1964-65), 379-387; 473-480; Richard A. McCormick S.J., "Adolescent Masturbation: A Pastoral Problem," *Homiletic and Pastoral Review* 60 (1959-60), 527-540.
5.
Anthony R. Kosnick, *The Imputability of Acts of Masturbation Among Males*, a doctoral dissertation, (Rome, 1961), 12. "For many non-Catholics masturbation constitutes no moral problem whatsoever." The author cites a number of references to substantiate his statement.

6.
J. G. Prick and J. A. Calon, "Masturbation Among Boys," *New Problems in Medical Ethics*, Vol. I, 37: These authors assume that the "onanism of puberty can be understood in the light of the very nature of the normal conditions of puberty." Von Gagern (p. 97) says, "Self-abuse is in accordance with normal development at their introverted stage of early puberty, for it is a symptom of immaturity."
7.
The authors mentioned in note 2 give detailed analyses of the causes or occasions of masturbation. E.g., Hagmaier-Gleason (p. 81): "Masturbation can mean many different things to different penitents." Van Gagern calls masturbation a symptom (p. 95).
8.
Hagmaier-Gleason, 75.
9.
Hagmaier-Gleason, 80.
10.
"The Pastoral Constitution on the Church in the Modern World," (*Gaudium et Spes*), n. 51.
11.
M. Flick S.J. and Z. Alszeghy S.J., "L'opzione fondamentale della vita morale e la grazia," *Gregorianum* 41 (1960), 593-619; Alszeghy-Flick, "Il peccato originale in prospettiva personalistica," *Gregorianum* 46 (1965), 705-732; J. J. Sikora S.J., "Faith and the First Moral Choice," *Sciences Ecclésiastiques* 17 (1965), 327-337. Further bibliography is given in these articles.
12.
Pierre Fransen S.J., "Toward a Psychology of Divine Grace," *Lumen Vitae* 12 (1957), 203-232.
13.
Alszeghy-Flick, *Gregorianum* 46 (1965), 705-732; John Hyde S.J., "Grace: A Bibliographical Note," *Irish Theological Quarterly* 32 (1964), 257-261.

14.

S. Lyonnet S.J., *Le Péché: Judaisme—Nouveau Testament—Péché Originel (Extrait du Supplément au Dictionnaire de la Bible* VII, col. 481-567). The rather lengthy extract, which summarizes many of Lyonnet's other articles and contains a complete bibliography, is available from the Pontifical Biblical Institute in Rome.

15.

Bernard Häring C.SS.R., *The Law of Christ*, Vol. I (Newman Press, 1961), 363. Also see A. Landgraf, *Das Wesen des lässlichen Sünde in der scholastik bis Thomas von Aquin* (Görresverlag, Bamberg, 1923); R. Blomme, *La doctrine du péché dans les écoles théologiques de la première moitié du XIIe siècle* (Louvain, 1958).

16.

Häring, 350-364, gives some of the reasons mentioned in the text. Although Häring does not employ the term "fundamental option," his whole exposition of the difference between mortal and venial sin is based on the reality which we have called the fundamental option.

17.

For the theory of the final option, see Ladislaus Boros S.J., *The Mystery of Death* (Herder and Herder, 1965); Roger Troisfontaines S.J., *I Do Not Die* (Desclee, 1963); Karl Rahner S.J., *On the Theology of Death* (Herder and Herder, 1961).

18.

Häring, 362, comes to the same conclusion. Häring deserves great credit as the first author of a general treatise of moral theology to treat sin in this way. Unfortunately, in his consideration of special moral theology Häring does not always carry through his theoretical consideration of the presumptive nature of grave and light matter. Of course, one must realize that Häring originally wrote his moral theology treatise over ten years ago.

19.

M. Huftier, "Péché mortel et péché véniel," *Théologie du*

péché, ed. Ph. Delhaye (Desclée, Tournai, 1960), 363-451;
C. Vogel, "Le péché et la penitence," *Pastorale du péché*
(Desclée, Tournai, 1961), 147-234.
20.
Dom Cyprian Stockford, "Sin, Hell and Sacraments," *The Downside Review* 81 (1963), 22-36.
21.
Huftier, 430-436.
22.
". . . est veniale ex genere propter materiam in qua peccatur.
In illa autem materia peccatum perfecte invenitur in qua,
si peccetur, virtus caritatis ad Deum et ad proximum dissol-
vitur, per quam vita est animae, et ideo quando aliquis peccat
in his sine quibus recte servatis non remanet subjectio homi-
nis ad Deum et foedus humanae societatis, tunc est peccatum
mortale ex genere." *In II Sent.*, dist. 42, q. 1, art. 4, in corp.
"Quaecumque igitur peccata intentioni ultimi finis et dilec-
tioni opponuntur, mortalia sunt." *Summa Contra Gentiles*,
1. 3, cap. 139.
23.
E.g., disobedience (*II II*, q. 105, a.1.); stealing (*II II*, q. 66,
a.6); injustice (*II II*, q. 59, a.4); sloth (*II II*, q. 35. a.3);
wrath (*II II*, q. 158, a.3); gluttony (*II II*, q. 148, a.2).
24.
Fuchs, 68; V. Vangheluwe, "De Intrinseca et Gravi Malitia
Pollutionis," *Collationes Brugenses* 48 (1952), 108-115.
25.
Dom Odon Lottin, *Morale Fondamentale* (Desclée, Tournai, 1954), 490.
26.
Fuchs, 68; Vangheluwe, 108-115.
27.
Since the Middle Ages and especially in the present century
there has been a development in the importance attached to
the love union aspect of sexuality. For the best historical consideration of the Church's teaching on marriage, see John T.
Noonan, Jr., *Contraception: A History of its Treatment by*

the Catholic Theologians and Canonists (Harvard University Press, 1965) .
28.
A. Lecomte, *L'Ovulation Spontanée* (Louvain, 1873) , 117.
29.
For a well balanced Protestant view of the relationship between the sexual faculty and the sexual act, see the response of R. Paul Ramsey in *The Vatican Council and the World of Today*, the proceedings of a conference held at Brown University, March 15, 1966, and prepared for publication by the Office of the Secretary of the University.
30.
Fuchs, 63, is typical of the approach of the modern manuals about the scriptural teaching on masturbation.
31.
The author is grateful to Ferenc Nagy S.J., for sending the conclusions of his unpublished doctoral dissertation (Pontifical Gregorian University) , which studied the evolution of the Church's teaching on masturbation in the first ten centuries. The author is also grateful to the students of his graduate seminar in the School of Theology of the Catholic University of America who did much historical research covering the same period.
32.
D.S. 688. The letter of Leo IX, *Ad Splendidum Nitentis* comments on a previous letter of Peter Damien, *Liber Gomorrhianus* (*P.L.* 145, col. 159-190) .
33.
A.A.S. 21 (1929) , 490, Pope XII, in an allocution on March 23, 1952, about the formation of a right conscience in youth, affirmed the gravity of the obligation in sexual matters even for adolescents and said it was erroneous to think that ordinarily passion takes away grave guilt (*A.A.S.* 44 (1952) , 270 ff.) . References condemning masturbation for medical purposes include *A.A.S.* 45 (1953) , 678 and *A.A.S.* 48 (1956) , 472, 473.

34.
Bernard Häring C.SS.R., at a two week institute for professors of moral theology at Regis College, Toronto, Canada, in July 1963, publicly defended as probable in practice the opinion that voluntary emission of the semen for medical purposes is not wrong.
35.
G. J. Waffelaert, *De Virtutibus Cardinalibus: De Prudentia, Fortitudine, et Temperantia* (Brugis, 1889), n. 187, 188, 302, 303. Arthurus Vermeersch S.J., *De Castitate et De Vitiis Contrariis* (Roma, 1919), 355 ff; Noonan, 358.
36.
Waffelaert, n. 187, 301.
37.
Waffelaert, n. 188, 303.
38.
For an historical study of the question of parvity of matter José M. Diaz S.J., "La doctrina moral sobre la parvedad de materia in re venerea desde Cayetano hasta San Alfonso," *Archivo Teologico Granadino* 23 (1960), 5-138.
39.
"The Dogmatic Constitution on the Church," (*Lumen Gentium*), n. 12; "The Declaration on Religious Freedom," (*Dignitatis Humanae*), n. 1. See also the extensive theological literature on the prophetic office in the Church.

Christian
Responsibility

Epilogue

This chapter will attempt to synthesize the various elements mentioned in the earlier chapters in an effort to arrive at a more unified understanding of the responsibilities of the Christian in contemporary life. The chapter will briefly show the meaning of Christian responsibility in three areas: responsibility in the world, responsibility in relation to Church law, and responsibility and absolute norms in moral theology.

RESPONSIBILITY IN THE WORLD

The horizons of man's responsibilities in a world come of age are constantly widening. The ethics of Jesus with his emphasis on openness and continual growth calls for ever-developing responsibilities. Man in the age of technology and science has a new opportunity to carry out the biblical mandate to subdue the earth. The reign of God is not entirely future; the reign of God is already present in this world. The Christian is called here and now to cooperate responsibly in bringing about the new heaven and the new earth. The social and cosmic aspects of the reign of God are more apparent than ever before. However, the call to conversion will never cease to demand a change of our own hearts. All the aspects of the reign of God must be seen together. To emphasize personal conversion to the exclusion of the social and cosmic aspect of the reign of God is just as unilateral and inadequate as an overemphasis on the social aspect of conversion while forgetting the need to change our hearts.

Man in a world come of age also needs to remember the Christian teaching about sin both as it continues to exist in our own hearts and in the political, social, and cultural structures of contemporary human existence. Now that Christians realize the cosmic aspect of creation and redemption, the followers of Jesus must also recall the cosmic aspect of sin. The prophets of the Old Testament inveighed against the social injustices of the times. Biblical thought has always seen some connection between sin and human suffering—especially in the form of poverty. Human avarice and selfishness are seen in the many attempts of the wealthy and powerful, both individuals and nations, to exploit the poor and the helpless. The gospel of John tells the story of the blind man who was cured by Jesus (John 9). Jesus corrected the mistaken notion that suffering was due to the man's personal sins or to the sins of his parents. But Jesus did not deny some connection between sin and human suffering. Today the contemporary Christian must be aware of the presence of sin in the world as well as in his own heart.

Catholic theology stresses the sacramental principle—the love and favor of God becomes visible and present through Jesus, the Church, and the sacraments. Sin too becomes visible in the world in which we live. Poverty and suffering in the world today are truly sacraments of sin. The avarice and selfishness of mankind become visible in the wants and deprivations of so many people. In a true sense, sin is the radical poverty of man. Poverty is usually defined in terms of human wants and human needs. Theology and many strains of contemporary philosophy teach that the greatest human want and need is for communion. However, sin is the radical breaking of our communion with God and neighbor. Man is made to live in a community of love, and sin separates him from such a union with God and neighbor. Sin is the radical poverty of man. The connection between sin and human poverty and misery is not merely rhetoric or metaphor. There is a real connection between sin and poverty. Human poverty and misery in the world is truly a sacrament of sin.

Many Christians tend to lose the sense of sin. All of us are tempted to forget and pass over the sinfulness which remains in our own hearts. The true Christian strives to be aware of the existence of sin in his own heart and in the world. The Christian call to conversion entails an unending struggle against the forces of sin. The presence of sin forms a constant reminder to the Christian of the need for continual growth and conversion. Sin always resists the approach of love. The follower of Jesus will experience the same opposition and frustration as his Master. Too many people today have a naive optimism and personalism which does not realize the frustration and opposition which will mark the life of the Christian. However, the Christian is not pessimistic. The resurrection is our hope. The Christian even now shares in the joy and victory of the Paschal Mystery as he continues the creating, redeeming, and reconciling work of God in time and space.

Responsibility calls for maturity on the part of the Christian in his approach to the problems of society and the world today. Problems of poverty and peace are complex; enthusiasm can never be a substitute for the competence which is required in all these areas. Change will not come about quickly. The Christian needs the active patience of the Paschal Mystery in trying to build the new heaven and the new earth. Likewise, it is not always easy to know and read the will of God in trying to find particular solutions to complex problems. Responsibility means a willingness to continue the efforts to find better solutions to the complex problems which face man today.

RESPONSIBILITY AND CHURCH LAWS

Responsibility also characterizes Catholic life in its relationship to the Canon Law of the Church. Chapter Four has pointed out the changed theological and sociological climate of life in the Church. More responsibility is now placed on individual initiative. The role of law is not to direct as much of the activity of the members as possible, but rather to create the climate so that individuals and smaller groups within the Church can better live their Christian lives and vocations. Tensions arise precisely because the canonical structure of the Church does not reflect the theological and sociological reality of life in the Catholic Church as we know it today.

The legislation of the Catholic Church on marriage and its indissolubility serves as an excellent illustration of the problem. Chapter One briefly discussed, from a theological viewpoint, the possibility of seeing the indissolubility of marriage as the goal toward which a Christian marriage strives while reluctantly admitting that some couples might not be able to live up to that ideal or goal. Our present consideration presupposes the teaching on the indissolubility of *ratum et consummatum* marriages but points out the tensions created by the fact that the canonical legislation appears to be inadequate and lacking in a number of areas. Such inadequate legislation would seem to be no longer binding. Pastors and couples today are often convinced that many marriages are invalid, but they cannot be proven to be invalid according to the present canonical discipline.

One of the major defects in the current legislation is the presumption, stated in Canon 1014, that marriage enjoys the favor of the law. Consequently, the marriage is valid unless the contrary can be proven with moral certitude.[1] Many times such certitude is lacking. The presumption in favor of the existence of the bond of marriage involves two aspects: (1) If the marriage was truly celebrated, the marriage is presumed valid unless its nullity is certainly proved. (2) Even if the celebration of marriage is not certain, the marriage is presumed to be valid if there exists "possession in favor of the existence of the marriage" (i.e., if openly it is thought to be a valid marriage). The main arguments for the present legislation, according to canonical interpreters, are the fear of breaking a divine law by dissolving a true marriage bond and the fact that the good of society demands such a presumption. Innocent III declared long ago that it is more tolerable to leave people married against the statutes of man than to separate legitimately married people against the statutes of God. Certain injustices may result from such a presumption, but the demands of the divine law and the good of society must be protected despite injustices which may occasionally be done to individuals.[2]

Is the presumption in favor of the existence of the bond and the need for a true moral certitude to overcome that presumption legitimate? I think not. In many other areas theology has shifted from an emphasis on divine law and the needs of society to an emphasis on the rights of the individual. The law has not kept pace with changed theological emphasis. In a former age theologians argued that the common good required the defendant to admit his crime to the judge. However, contemporary theologians uphold the right of the defendant to keep silent when interrogated about his guilt. Canon law itself now recognizes the defendant's right to silence (Canon 1743 § 1).

The controversy over religious liberty shows another change of emphasis from the demands of divine law and the common good of society to the rights of the individual. Previously it was argued that the divine law for all men to worship God in the one, true Church would always take precedence over the freedom of the individual to worship God according to the dictates of his own conscience. One could see how the words of Innocent III would have applied in this situation. It would be more tolerable for religious freedom to be denied to people than have people violate God's law of worshiping in the one, true Church. Also, an older mentality thought that the common good demanded a unity in religious practice. Today we know this is not true. The defenders of the present presumption in favor of marriages can argue that the common good demands that the indissolubility of marriage always have the benefit of the doubt. However, I do not think that one can say the common good is always better served by the need to prove the invalidity of the marriage bond with moral certitude. The common good would seem to be better served by giving as much freedom as possible to the individual and his rights. All three cases are not completely *a pari*. However, the general thrust in theology and law is to give as much leeway as possible to the freedom of the individual. At least, the individual should not always be forced to prove the invalidity of a marriage with rather strict moral certitude when "there is a positive and probable doubt, that is, reasons both for validity and against it."[3] The tension between the Code of Canon Law and contemporary life stems from the fact that the legislation does not seem to be in keeping with the current emphasis, recognized elsewhere in theology and canon law, on the rights of the individual.

The argument about the presumption in favor of the existence of the bond is not merely theoretical and esoteric. There are many marriages in which couples are morally convinced there is no valid bond, but the nonexistence of the bond cannot be proved with the degree of proof presently required in the Code. Think, for example, of teen-age marriages; marriages in war time; marriages entered into because of duress; marriages in which the person did not seem to have the requisite psychological maturity for such a decision; marriages in which the couples separated after a comparatively short time (e.g., one year), thus casting doubt on the validity of the marriage from the very beginning.

The current matrimonial legislation is also inadequate because the whole psychological aspect of human relations receives practically no consideration. In judging the morality of masturbation, the point was already made that the older judgments were inaccurate because of a unilateral approach solely in terms of the biological and physical aspects of masturbation. In questions concerning the indissolubility of marriage, consummation has been defined purely in physical terms. Is physical consummation all that is required to have a consummated marriage? Is there not also necessary some type of psychological consummation? A breakdown of the marriage soon after the wedding might be a very good indication that there was no true consummation of the marriage. Psychological notions also deserve a greater hearing in questions concerning the necessary consent for marriage. The impediments of marriage, reflecting a long canonical history, do not specifically mention psychological factors. Physical impotency is a diriment impediment, but no mention is made of psychological incompatibility in any form.

Certainly some forms of psychological illness or sexual aber-
rations (e.g., true homosexuality of one of the partners)
should at least have an effect on the necessary consent for
marriage if they would not in themselves constitute impediments.

There are inadequacies in the canonical legislation on
marriage which call for reform. In the meantime, the tensions will continue to grow. What can be done when a person is morally convinced there is no previous marital bond
but cannot prove it according to the current legislation? In
such cases, I believe that the individuals are free to contract
a true marriage in the eyes of God. Current legislation forbids any legal marriage ceremony which is recognized by the
Church in the external forum. However, a couple entering
such a marriage would be under no excommunication, such
as the excommunication of the Third Council of Baltimore
for those who attempt marriage after civil divorce. Excommunication as a penalty presupposes a grave crime (Canons
2214-2219). The canonical axiom says: *nulla poena sine
delicto*. A penalty presupposes a crime which in turn presupposes grave culpability on the part of the person (Canon
2195). Since there is no moral culpability in entering a
marriage when one is convinced there is no previous bond,
there can be no canonical penalty. At most, one could argue
that on the basis of the presumption those in charge of the
external forum of the Church could act upon the presumed
existence of an excommunication. The couple, however,
would always retain their right to participate fully in the
eucharistic life of the Church. A couple now living in an
"invalid marriage" might also be truly married in the eyes
of God because they cannot legally prove, in accord with the
required prescriptions, the invalidity of a previous bond.
Such a couple should also feel free to participate in the
sacramental life of the Church.

The discussion has been limited to inadequacies in canonical legislation within the framework of the indissolubility of *ratum et consummatum marriages*. Pastoral experience seems to indicate the existence of a great number of marriages in which an objective observer is convinced there is no valid bond, but the fact of invalidity cannot be proven according to the legislation in the Code of Canon Law. The larger question of the indissolubility of marriage has not been considered. However, on a pastoral level one could apply to the problem of the ecclesiastical unworthiness of a person in an invalid marriage the fact that such a person may not have committed grave sin and thus may not have contracted an ecclesiastical censure. Every person involved in such an invalid second marriage would not seem to be absolutely excluded from the sacramental life of the Church.[4]

RESPONSIBILITY AND ABSOLUTE NORMS

The greatest area of dispute in contemporary moral theology and Christian ethics centers on the issue of situation ethics or the role of principles and context in moral theology. The question is phrased in different ways, but the basic problem revolves around the existence of specific, negative, universal norms of moral conduct. All sides in the debate will naturally claim responsibility for their viewpoint. In the interests of seeking the truth such emotionally charged words should not be employed without definite supporting proof. The general thrust of many of these chapters is in the direction of diminishing the number of such absolute norms in moral theology. However, criticisms of the situation ethics espoused by Joseph Fletcher were also given.

The problems raised by the question of situation ethics are many and complex. In such a debate one must be cognizant of complexity and not accept overly simplistic solutions. In view of the complexity of the question, James M. Gustafson has argued that a debate in terms of context *versus* principles is misplaced because most ethical systems employ some principles (at least a first principle) and the context, as well as other elements. The problem is one of emphasis and correlation rather than a simplistic either-or.[5] Catholic moral theology has been characterized by an emphasis on absolute norms. The contention of the preceding chapters is that specific absolutes in moral theology should be much fewer than they have been in the past. Without even attempting to solve the complex question of situation ethics, the argument has been advanced for reducing the emphasis on such norms.

There are both theological and philosophical reasons for questioning and denying some of the absolute norms which have been proposed in the manuals of moral theology. The theological reasons mentioned in the preceding chapters are the possibility of absolutizing an ethical ideal as in the case of divorce and a tendency to forget the existence and influence of sin in Christian decision-making. One of the reasons why the manuals of Catholic theology did not give sufficient attention to the presence and influence of sin was a poor— and now abandoned—concept of nature and grace. Grace is a superstructure added to the substructure of nature. Sin toppled the superstructure of grace but left nature intact. Man after the fall into sin was compared to a man existing in the hypothetical state of pure nature as *nudatus ad nudum*. Both are now nude; the only difference being that previously the sinner had clothing. Sin did not really affect the nature of man. However, there were other aspects of Catholic theology which did show an effect of sin on man's nature; e.g., the axiom that sin left man wounded in those things pertaining to nature. Theologians today have a better idea of the nature-grace relationship. Grace is not seen as a superstructure

added to nature. Most contemporary Catholic theologians
would agree with a concept of Christ transforming culture
and nature as proposed by H. Richard Niebuhr rather than
a concept of Christ adding to nature and culture.[6] Catholic
theology today realizes the presence of sin and speaks of the
cosmic and social dimension of sin in the world. The presence of sin in the world means that the Christian will occasionally fall short of what he might want to do under more
ideal circumstances. A theology of compromise was proposed
to deal with the ambiguities proposed by the existence of sin
in the world.

Perhaps the viewpoint of Roman Catholic moral theology
has also tended to avoid the reality and influence of sin in
Christian decision-making. Moral theology considers the human action from the viewpoint of a third person (the judge)
objectively viewing the particular action in a rather abstract
manner. If the viewpoint of considering the action placed
more emphasis on the person's assuming responsibility for
his own action, then the influence of sin might have received
greater attention. Notice that my approach to the theory of
compromise started from the subjective viewpoint and not
the objective (i.e., Catholic theology has always admitted the
influence of sin and other limitations on the voluntariness
of the human action). The theory of compromise thus tries
to overcome the one-sided approach (the somewhat abstract
judgment of another person) which has characterized the
moral theology of the manuals.

However, the basic problem in the debate over situation
ethics in the Catholic tradition centers on philosophical and
not theological grounds. Here again I believe the debate has
been misplaced. The general tone of most Catholic defenders
of the absolute norms of the moral manuals has put the debate in too simplistic terms. It was a question of either a sub-
jectivistic existentialist ethic or the absolute norms based on

the understanding of natural law as explained in the manuals of theology. Any attempt to abandon the already existing absolute norms was looked upon as a subjective ethic which was no longer based on reality and objective norms.[7] The contention of the previous chapters has been that morality should be based on reality, but reality may be viewed differently from the approach taken in the manuals of moral theology. It is much too simplistic to reduce the entire debate to either a subjective ethic or the existence of such absolute norms as has always been taught in moral theology.

Two chapters have insisted on a more historical methodology in moral theology as opposed to the more classicist methodology. The different methodologies are related to different worldviews and different understandings of reality. A more historical understanding of reality can still claim to be a realistic ethic and yet seriously question a number of the absolute norms previously accepted in Catholic moral theology. A classicist worldview tends to see reality in terms of individual substances which are constituted in themselves and admit of only accidental growth and change. The historical worldview accepts a greater amount of plasticity and growth. The substance is not completely constituted in itself independently of relationships with the rest of reality. An historical worldview is more sympathetic to a relational rather than a substantialist view of reality.

A substantialist view considers everything as an independent substance already constituted in itself and merely accidentally related with other beings and persons. For Aristotle, relation is an accident and the weakest of all being. Every substance has within it a nature or principle of operation which determines the future development of the being. The future is already inscribed in the nature present in the reality. Thus growth and change are severely limited and in a sense already contained within the substance. Such a substantialist view also seems to have affected the viewpoints of Catholic theology on scientific methodology and the complicated question of the development of doctrine. In scientific methodology, a substantialist view of reality is closely aligned with a deductive approach. Everything is already contained in the premise; one just has to make explicit and extricate from the major premise by logical reasoning what is already contained therein. In the question of development, a substantialist view admits only an accidental development without any essential change. The newer understanding is already contained in the old and can be derived from the former teaching by logical processes.

A more relational view of reality does not see every individual reality as totally constituted in itself. Rather, a being is what it is precisely because of its relationship with other beings and the fullness of being. A being is constituted by its relationships. A more relational approach does not expect to find within the thing itself a detailed plan for its future growth and development. Growth and change are something more than merely making explicit what is already present in the substance itself. A substantialist view would define person as a *subsistens distinctum in natura intellectuali*. A more relational view would tend to see the person as constituted in and through his relationships with other persons and reality.

The moral methodology employed by a substantialist approach definitely differs from the approach of a more relational understanding of reality. A substantialist approach examines the particular substance or faculty. A particular substance or faculty is so constituted that it should always function in a definite way. If it functions in a way contrary to the purpose engraved in its own being, then the action is against nature and wrong. Take, for example, the question of lying which was mentioned earlier. A substantialist approach

looks at the faculty of speech, determines what is the purpose
and function of the faculty of speech, and thus arrives at a
norm for determining the moral use of the faculty of speech.
The faculty of speech exists to express thoughts which are in
man's mind. A lie as an immoral use of the faculty occurs
when speech expresses something which is contrary to what
is in the speaker's mind. One determines the morality of the
action simply by applying the norm acquired from an understanding of the purpose of the faculty seen in itself.

Theologians, in general, no longer define a lie in relation
to the purpose of the faculty of speech. Lying is defined in a
more relational manner as a violation of my neighbor's right
to truth or as an action which is destructive of the trust and
confidence necessary for community.[9] Actually, Augustine at
first proposed the notion of lying that is now becoming more
acceptable among theologians. Such a definition is more relational because a lie is defined in terms of a man's relationship to the person or persons with whom he is talking and
to the entire community. In the former definition in which
lying is determined by the norm of the purpose of the faculty, one can easily and readily determine what is a lie. The
norm is very concrete and clear. In a more relational understanding there are many more factors (namely, relations)
which have to be considered before one can judge that such
an action is a lie. Only in the given situation can one examine all the various relationships and come to the conclusion
that an action is a lie. The contemporary understanding of
lying admits the distinction between falsehood and lying. A
falsehood is a word which is not in conformity with what is
in the mind. However, not every falsehood is a lie. The malice of lying is determined only by a more relational approach
examining the neighbor's right to truth and the community
building or destroying aspects of the action. The older definition of a lie was much more absolute because it was always

true that a lie was a word not in conformity with the mind. A relational understanding of lying is "less absolute" and precise because lying can now be identified only in relation to my neighbor's right to truth.

A second defect in the traditional manualistic natural law approach is the tendency to identify the physical aspect of the action with the full moral meaning of the action. Such a viewpoint definitely was more in accord with a non-technical and non-scientific world. Today, however, man through technology constantly interferes in the process of nature to humanize nature and bring it more under man's domain. The moral action, however, cannot be identified merely with a physical process of nature. Generally, Catholic moral theology has avoided the danger of identifying the moral action with the physical substratum of the action. Theologians now admit the difference between the physical action of falsehood and the moral action of lying. Likewise, a distinction is made between the physical action of taking something and the moral action of stealing. The physical action of killing is distinguished from the moral action of murder. However, in the area of medical ethics morality is still frequently based on the physical structure of the act alone. Problems of contraception, sterilization, masturbation for seminal analysis, artificial insemination, mutilation, and others, have been solved by identifying the total human and moral action with the merely physical aspect of the action.

The problem of identifying the human action with the physical structure of the action is also apparent in the understanding of the notion of the direct and indirect voluntary in the manuals of theology. Catholic theology has tried to solve conflict situations through the understanding of the direct and indirect effect of human actions. The distinction between direct and indirect has been invoked to solve the complicated moral problems of killing of self or others, abortion, sterilization, mutilation, etc. However, I believe the understanding of direct and indirect as found in some manuals of moral theology is inadequate precisely because of a tendency to identify the human action in terms of the physical structure of the action. Some writers maintain that the basis of the distinction is to be found solely in the nature of the action itself. For example, direct killing is an action which is *per se occisiva* or an action whose *finis operis* is killing.[10] Catholic moralists have generally agreed that when the sole immediate effect of the action is killing the action is direct killing and therefore wrong.[11]

An example of abortion will show the inadequacy of an understanding of direct based on the sole immediate effect of the action. Take the hypothetical case of a woman who is told by competent medical authority that she is now pregnant but will be unable to bring the child to term. According to the best available medical knowledge, the fetus will not be able to be born and live. Also, if the mother does continue to carry the fetus for a number of months she will seriously jeodardize her own life. A manualist approach would say that the abortion of the fetus now would be a direct abortion because the sole immediate effect of the action is the killing of the fetus. No matter how laudatory the purpose of the action, the abortion is direct and wrong. In this case, the incongruity of basing the moral decision on the physical action seen in itself is evident. The fetus, according to the best available medical knowledge, cannot be born alive. Since the fetus will die in the future and since in the meantime the life of the mother is being threatened, why cannot the doctor now interfere to abort the fetus? Medical science has given man the opportunity to interfere with nature and not just to sit back and wait for nature to run its course. I do not think that the ultimate moral decision in complex circumtances can be decided on the basis of the physical structure of an action and the sole, immediate, physical effect of an action. All the moral values must be considered and a final decision made after all the moral values have been compared.

One of the main problems connected with abortion is the determination of when human life begins. I firmly oppose any insinuation that the fetus is merely tissue or a part of the mother. There are some arguments against the fetus as human life (e.g., the conscientious experience of many people of good will, the number of fertilized ova that are spontaneously aborted without the mother's knowledge of it). However, the proponents of the argument that the fetus is not human life have not been able to show any logical difference between abortion and infanticide or other forms of taking life. If one wants to define human personhood in terms of the socialization process or interpersonal relations, then there are many persons outside the womb who would not be persons according to those definitions and descriptions. The problem is very complicated and far beyond the scope of this chapter. In general, I believe that the fetus (or the fertilized ovum from the very beginning) is a genetic package which is at least in close continuity with human life. At the present time, I conclude that from the time of blastocyst (about eight days[?] after fertilization) the fetus must be considered as human life.

A Christian moralist tends to be conservative in dealing with human life. Life is the greatest gift that man has received from God. However, Christians have always admitted the existence of conflict situations in which it might be a necessity, albeit reluctant, to take the life of a human person. Catholic moral theology has generally solved the conflict situations involving abortion by an application of the principle of direct and indirect effects. It is erroneous to say that

Catholic teaching is opposed to all abortion. Catholic theology has never made the life of the fetus an absolute value which can never be taken under any circumstances.

Moral theology permits an indirect abortion. Two examamples of indirect abortion involve the removal of an ectopic pregnancy and the removal of a cancerous uterus which contains a fetus.[12] Earlier, we considered the notion of the direct effect as being determined by the sole immediate effect of the action. A fuller description of direct is presented by one moral theologian in this vein: "Direct is that which is intended in itself as an end or as a means either explicitly or implicitly so that the action or omission is able to tend immediately to no other end."[13] In the case of the ectopic pregnancy the action tends to removing a pathological organ (e.g. the tube) which happens to contain a fetus. The same is true of the removal of a cancerous uterus which happens to contain a fetus. The action in neither case tends immediately to the expulsion of the fetus but to the curing of a pathological condition. Some theologians have proposed as a rule of thumb that the abortion is indirect if the action could be done without killing the fetus or if the procedure would be done if the fetus is present or not.[14] The pathological tube or the cancerous womb would be removed even if there were no fetus present. Thus the action tends not to the expulsion of the fetus but to another end, the curing of a pathological condition.

Does the theory of direct and indirect abortion adequately solve the problems presented by the conflict situations involving the life of the fetus? In general, I do not believe that the theory of direct and indirect as described above adequately comes to grips with all the problems of conflict situations involving the fetus. It seems that, in accord with such a principle, moral theology has attributed a more absolute value to life inside the womb than to life outside the womb. Moral theologians traditionally deny that the fetus can be an unjust aggressor. However, outside the womb a drunken person or an insane person can be an unjust aggressor and forfeit his right to live even though he is in no way responsible for the aggression he is performing. A human person outside the womb can be a materially unjust aggressor, but life in the womb cannot be such a materially unjust aggressor.[15]

There is in moral theology another instance of conflict situations involving human life in which the proposed solutions are wider than in the case of abortion. St. Thomas asked the question if a person could kill another in defending himself. Thomas replied in the affirmative by applying the principle that governs an act having two effects. Actions receive their moral species according to what is intended. In this case one intends the preservation of his life. Since one intends the good effect, the act is licit provided that the act is proportionate to the end in view (*II II*, q. 64 a. 7). Thomas' understanding would seem to be much wider than the application of direct and indirect to abortion according to the manuals of moral theology. Thomas appears to say that in defending oneself the action of defense, as such, does not enter into the picture as constituent of morality. Logically, one could defend craniotomy to preserve the life of the mother according to the principles of Thomas even though moral theologians and Church statements deny the morality of craniotomy in those cases.[16]

Subsequent theologians have referred to the passage of St. Thomas in treating the question of self-defense against unjust aggression. Notice that the passage from Thomas does not explicitly speak of unjust aggression. Some theologians follow Thomas and say that killing an unjust aggressor in self-defense is indirect killing because the agent intends to defend himself.[17] Other Catholic theologians follow the opinion of Lessius and De Lugo in maintaining that killing in such cases is direct. These theologians fail to see how one can avoid the conclusion that the person intends to kill his assailant as a means of defending himself. For example, Zalba believes that killing an unjust aggressor cannot be solved on the basis of the principles of the double effect, but must be seen as a legitimate means to use in the protection of one's rights.[18] Thus in the case of unjust aggression theologians either accept an understanding of direct and indirect that does not depend on the physical structure of the act or some theologians admit the need for a principle other than the principle of the double effect to solve the problems created by the conflict situation.

Conflict situations involving human life and the more specific cases of unjust aggression have been solved in a manner different from the solution to conflict cases in abortion with the emphasis on the physical structure and causality of the action itself. Logically, one could argue that abortion to save the life of the mother might also be justified in certain circumstances even though the immediate end of the action was the expulsion of the fetus.

The casuistry involved in the question of unjust aggression illustrates that Catholic theology has been willing in the past to equate other values on a par with life itself. Even contemporary theologians admit many other values, such as spiritual and material goods of great importance, can be defended even to the extent of killing the assailant.[19] Frankly, I think the casuists have stretched the values proportionate to taking life to too great an extreme. However, in this area Catholic theology has taught that other goods are proportionate to the value of human life.

In discussing the problem of abortion I believe that a Christian theologian must take the conservative position of treating the fetus at least from blastocyst as human life. However, in the past the teaching of Catholic theologians and the statements of the hierarchical magisterium on abortion seem too restricted. Conflict situations cannot be solved merely by the physical structure and causality of the act. The human values involved must be carefully considered and weighed. In Catholic theology there is a precedent for equating other values with life itself. As a Christian, any taking of life must be seen as a reluctant necessity. However, in the case of abortion there can arise circumstances in which the abortion is justified for preserving the life of the mother or for some other important value commensurate with life even though the action itself aims at abortion "as a means to the end." One cannot stress enough the great respect the Christian has for human life. Human life can never be taken lightly. However, the conflict situation involving abortion should be solved according to the pattern and model of other conflict situations involving life and not solved merely according to a restricted notion of direct or indirect based on the physical causality of the action itself. Other contemporary Catholic theologians seem to be in accord, at least in principle, with the thought expressed in the above paragraphs.[20]

A third defect in the manualistic understanding of reality and objective morality has been a rather "picture-book concept of reality." This concept has much in common with the defect of identifying the human action with the physical structure of the action. A realistic epistomology does not necessarily have to be based on the analogy of sense knowledge. The objectivity of human knowing is not the same as the objectivity of sense experience. Lonergan claims that the naive realists identify the objectivity and validity of human knowing with merely one component (sense perception) in the human knowing process. The objectivity of human knowing is always compared to the objectivity of the eye's visual perception of reality.[21] The dynamic structure of objective knowing does not merely discover the truth of the object. Man himself changes reality by adding meaning to it. The subject gives meaning to the object. Man's understanding of state, community, family, etc., enters into the reality of such terms. Objective knowing is not merely corresponding to the reality "out there."[22]

One of the criticisms of Catholic moral theology has been the understanding of intrinsic morality. Yes, I believe that morality must be objective and realistic; but this does not mean that all morality is contained in the object looked at in itself according to the analogy of vision. Man and the world are in dialogue with one another. Man gives meaning to reality and changes it. The manualistic notions of subjective and objective occasionally seem to suffer from the inadequacies of a naive realism. Modern art or cinema illustrate the meaning that man puts upon external reality. Modern art is not "objective," but more "subjective." The artist tries to express his own feelings and attitudes in the picture. The work of art is objective in the sense of expressing the reality the artist tries to express, but it is not objective in the sense of the objectivity of vision grasping the object which is entirely "out there." Morality can still be intrinsic, objective, and realistic without necessarily being identified with the physical and sensible aspects of reality.

The defects mentioned in the manualistic concept of natural law center on the identification of the moral, human action with the physical and external aspects of that action. One cannot point to a particular physical action and say it is always wrong. For example, one cannot say that falsehood (a merely physical reality) is always morally wrong. A moral methodology must be developed which sees the morality of actions not merely in terms of the nature and purposes of individual faculties or substances but rather in relation to other beings and persons. The physical aspect of an action is not always identifiable with the moral aspect of that action. A better understanding of reality argues for a more relational (if you want, contextual) emphasis in the methodological approach of moral theology.

A more relational methodology weighs all the different values involved in the situation. There may be times, as mentioned previously, when direct killing or direct abortion (defined as the sole immediate effect of the action) is a reluctant necessity and hence moral. There may be complicated situations in which one cannot know with any degree of certitude whether direct killing (as defined above) is right or wrong. For example, the prisoner of war who kills himself because he realizes that under torture he will reveal secrets detrimental to the lives of many others. The fact that the Church or theologians cannot say that a particular external action is always wrong reflects the complexity of reality and the imperfections of the pilgrim Christian. Paul Ramsey, a Protestant theologian, has praised the Pastoral Constitution on the Church in the Modern World because it did not attempt to give specific solutions for very complicated moral problems such as the Viet Nam war.[23] However, a relational approach to morality argues for complexity even in personal moral decisions. A relational moral approach does not advocate "pure subjectivism," but rather calls to mind that moral reality is not always identified with the physical structure of an action.

Notes for Epilogue

1.
"The constant practice of the Roman Curia in dealing with marriage cases is in strict accord with this principle. Subject to the exception about to be noted, in all cases where the evidence for nullity is not conclusive, the decision is: *non constare de nullitate;* that is, the presumption in favor of validity has not been overcome by contrary evidence." T.

Lincoln Bouscaren S.J., and Adam C. Ellis S.J., *Canon Law: A Text and Commentary* (Bruce, 1955), 459. However, Roman Law and earlier canon law used *fides* as the word to describe the type of proof necessary. *Fides* appears to be a less restrictive term than moral certitude.
2.
The paragraph has summarized the ideas presented by Felix M. Cappello S.I., *De Sacramentis V: De Matrimonio*, 7th ed. (Marietti, Rome, 1961), 44-47, and Eduardus F. Regatillo S.I., *Ius Sacramentarium*, 3rd ed. (Sal Terrae, Santander, Spain, 1960), 587-588.
3.
The quotation is an explanation of what is required according to Canon 1014 in the intepretation of Bouscaren-Ellis, 458.
4.
For a fuller discussion, see B. Peters, T. Beemer, and C. van der Poel, "Cohabitation in a 'Marital State of Mind,'" *Homiletic and Pastoral Review*, 66 (April 1966), 566-567. In Vol. 67 (February 1967) *Homiletic and Pastoral Review* carried the notice of a formal *monitum* in which the Sacred Congregation for the Doctrine of the Faith disapproved of the ideas advanced in the earlier article (p. 390). For a theological critique of the article by Peters *et al.*, see Richard A. McCormick S.J., "Notes on Moral Theology," *Theological Studies*, 27 (1966), 622-624. Notice that the *monitum* from the Congregation gave no specific reasons for rejecting the opinions proposed in the article. The lack of specific reasons and other circumstances surrounding the *monitum* appear to be inconsistent with the procedures to be followed by the Congregation for the Doctrine of the Faith as set down in the *Motu Proprio, Integrae Servandae*, issued by Pope Paul VI on December 7, 1965.
5.
James M. Gustafson, "Context Versus Principles: A Misplaced Debate in Christian Ethics," *Harvard Theological Review*, 58 (1965), 171-202.

6.
H. Richard Niebuhr, *Christ and Culture* (Harper and Row, 1951; Harper Torchbook, 1956). Aquinas' position is explained, pp. 128-141.

7.
E.g., Instruction of The Holy Office, February 2, 1956, *A.A.S.*, 48 (1956), 144 ff.; Karl Rahner S.J., "On the Question of a Formal Existential Ethic," *Theological Investigations*, Vol. II (Helicon, 1963), 217-234; Aidan M. Carr O.F.M.Conv., "The Morality of Situation Ethics," *Proceedings of the Catholic Theological Society of America*, 12 (1957), 75-102.

8.
An historical worldview is not totally incompatible with the best insights of St. Thomas. Process theologians such as Dewart and E. R. Baltazar would reject the approach of Thomas; whereas Marechal, Rahner, Murray, Lonergan, and others, would even claim to be following somewhat in the footsteps of Thomas.

9.
J. A. Dorszynski, *Catholic Teaching About the Morality of Falsehood* (The Catholic University of America Press, 1949).

10.
John McCarthy, *Problems in Theology II: The Commandments* (Newman Press, 1960), 119-122.

11.
Pope Pius XII defined the direct disposing of human life as "an action which aims at its destruction, whether such destruction be intended as an end or as a means toward some other end. . ." *A.A.S.*, 43 (1951), 838. McCarthy admits that the statement in our text would be the common teaching among Catholic moralists.

12.
E.g., Gerald Kelly S.J., *Medico-Moral Problems* (The Catholic Hospital Association, 1958), 62-110; Thomas J. O'Don-

nell S.J., *Morals in Medicine* (Newman Press, 1959), 153-235.
13.
Benedictus H. Merkelbach O.P., *Summa Theologiae Moralis II: De Virtutibus Moralibus*, 10th ed. (Desclée de Brouwer, Bruges, 1956), n. 349, p. 350.
14.
Arthur Vermeersch S.J., "Une corte conclusion," *Nouvelle Revue Theologique*, 60 (1938), 693. This article is in the context of a dispute between Vermeersch and Agostino Gemelli about the meaning of direct and indirect; Gerald Kelly S.J. and John Ford S.J., "Notes on Moral Theology," *Theological Studies*, 15 (1954), 68-71.
15.
The authors mentioned in note 12 exemplify the generally accepted teaching among Catholic moralists that the fetus cannot be considered as an unjust aggressor. Note well that the different approach to the conflict situation involving abortion which is proposed in the following paragraphs does not rise or fall on the fact that the fetus in the womb can be an unjust aggressor. I am just using this to show the apparent inconsistency in the present teaching which attributes a more absolute value to life existing inside the womb than to life existing outside the womb. There are other possible ways in which one could question the present teaching on abortion. My contention is that the solution of conflict cases based on an application of the principle of the indirect voluntary is inadequate precisely because the morality is determined merely by the physical structure of the act itself.
16.
Kelly, 69-75.
17.
Merkelbach, n. 361, pp. 362-364.
18.
Marcellino Zalba S.J., *Theologiae Moralis Summa II: De Mandatis Dei et Ecclesiae* (Biblioteca de Autores Cristianos, Madrid, 1953), 275-279.

Christian Responsibility 249

Merkelbach, 364, 365; Zalba, 275, 277. These theologians are truly representative of Catholic moral theologians on these issues.
20.
P. Knauer S.J., "La détermination du bien et du mal morale par le principe du double effet," *Nouvelle Revue Théologique*, 87 (1965), 356-376; W. van der Marck O.P., *Love and Fertility* (Sheed and Ward, London, 1965), 35-63; M. van Vyve, "La Mort Volontaire," *Revue Philosophique de Louvain*, 49 (1951), 78-107.
21.
Bernard Lonergan S.J., "Cognitional Structure," in *Collection* (Herder and Herder, 1967), 221-239.
22.
Lonergan, "Dimensions of Meaning," *Collection*, 252-267.
23.
Paul Ramsey, *Who Speaks for the Church?* (Abingdon Press, 1967), 124-147.